Praise for Ready

"*Ready* is the antidote to one of the most common crossroads we all experience as human beings—knowing when it is truly time to stay or go. Let this insightful guide support you in learning the language of readiness and cuing the courage required to make the big changes you seek."
—Amanda Gilbert, author of *Kindness Now*

"*Ready* posits that making important decisions is not about drawing up lists of pros and cons, consulting experts, or honing your willpower. Rather, it is about knowing yourself deeply, inhabiting each moment fully, and then letting the world speak to you in its infinite wisdom (which is not separate from your own). If you're looking for a way to make decisions you can trust, this book is for you."
—Susan Piver, author of *The Four Noble Truths of Love*

"*Ready* is a superbly succinct guide through the entanglements of fear, doubt, regret, and grief to a deepening trust of our decisions about our commitments and the skills needed to time them exquisitely. The journey through the practices is to be expertly companioned by a wise elder and a caring friend."
—Linda Graham, MFT, author of *Resilience*

Ready

HOW TO KNOW WHEN TO GO
AND WHEN TO STAY

David Richo

SHAMBHALA

Shambhala Publications, Inc.
2129 13th Street
Boulder, Colorado 80302
www.shambhala.com

Cover art: Gyzele/iStock and Ihor Biliavskyi/iStock
Cover design: Amanda Weiss
Interior design: Kate Huber-Parker

9 8 7 6 5 4 3 2 1

First Edition
Printed in the United States of America

♾ This edition is printed on acid-free paper that meets the
American National Standards Institute z39.48 Standard.
♻ This book is printed on 30% postconsumer recycled paper.
For more information please visit www.shambhala.com.
Shambhala Publications is distributed worldwide by
Penguin Random House, Inc., and its subsidiaries.

Library of Congress Cataloging-in-Publication Data
Names: Richo, David, 1940– author.
Title: Ready: how to know when to go and when to stay / David Richo.
Description: Boulder, Colorado: Shambhala, [2022]
Identifiers: LCCN 2021049685 | ISBN 9781611809497 (trade paperback)
Subjects: LCSH: Time—Psychological aspects. | Decision making. |
Change (Psychology)
Classification: LCC BF637.T5.R53 2022 | DDC 158—dc23/eng/20211117
LC record available at https://lccn.loc.gov/2021049685

To all of you
I so loved being with when I was at
St. Mary's in Greenwich, 1966–1968.

I still and always hold you in my heart.

Contents

Ready

Introduction

Why did I remain in that relationship for so long?
What kept me tied to my addiction all that time?
Why did I stay stuck in that job so many years?
How did I put up with being treated that way?
What got me so petrified that I couldn't go?
When I was already losing, why was I willing to
keep losing even more?
When that situation no longer fit for me, why
wouldn't I leave it?
When the only thing left was still not enough,
why did I settle for crumbs?
Why have I lingered so long in the Land of Less?

In more than fifty years as a psychotherapist, I have found that one issue has come up with clients more often than any other: staying too long in what doesn't work. I have done this too. Maybe everyone has? This "what doesn't work" can apply to relationships, jobs, predicaments, addictions, physical pain, unresolved conflicts, enmeshment in family drama, or affiliation to a religion, organization, or institution—just about anything we become involved in. We might be just as afraid to leave our discomfort zone as we are to leave our comfort zone! Our challenge is to know when it is time to go and then act on what we know.

On the other hand, there are times in life when we don't stay long enough. We don't hang in there through thick and thin in a relationship or affiliation that really *can* work. Our challenge, then, is to know when it is time to stay long enough to upgrade our connection so that it works.

This book is about both options in our human story: not staying too long in what doesn't work and staying long enough in what can. We will discover the fascinating connection these topics have to who we are and how we got to be that way.

Central to questions of staying and leaving is a third focus. And on it all depends: the mystery of timing. *Timing* in this book refers to timeliness, the opportune time, what is timely, what we mean when we say: "The time has come." Why we stay when it's time to go or go when it's time to stay is not entirely about choice and action. We wonder what makes us able to take action on a Monday rather than on a Sunday or Tuesday? Some clock lodged deeply within us tells us exactly when we are ready to go or even when to know we need to go. To hurry ourselves—or to linger—does not work if that inner timing is off. We can't jump the gun on Sunday. We can't lag till Tuesday. Everything real in life has to pass the test of time; nothing can override it.

Ultimately, we only go or stay when we are ready to do so. Our readiness depends on the ping of a timer not in our hands. Indeed, time is a player in all our comings and goings. This book helps us respond to our own perfect timing for the important decisions in life and then act in accord with that timing. We then reach the new world where never a gate slams shut nor a door is ever locked. These are the everywhere Dharma gates that never close. *Dharma* refers to the enlightened teachings of Buddha.

Self-help books and teachers may give the impression that we can take care of staying or going by jump-starting ourselves, taking action right away, snapping to it or out of it, using a technique that will hurl us into our next chapter. These strategies can sometimes work. But there is something else that has to be taken into account, an insoluble enigma to all of us: individual readiness, the other portrait in the locket of timing. Timing is not magic. It does not make us move. But it does help us activate when we are attuned to its gong. That attuning is readying ourselves. Readiness to stay or go means that:

- We see what's going on.
- We are prepared, fit to take action.
- We are equipped with what it takes to make our move.
- We are willing to act.

We understand our topic of readiness for movement best when we consider two possibilities: The first is we can't go because the timing is not right, a stubborn fact we have to respect. We are not ready to wake up because no bugle has sounded reveille, at least not yet.

The second possibility is not going when the timing is right. We disregard the inner alarm clock that shouts "Wake up!" Instead, we go back to sleep. To be stuck can mean not being ready for choice and movement when their time has indeed come. Then what we aren't changing, we are choosing. We are caught in inertia; a body at rest tends to stay at rest. Here is a summary of how each of the two possibilities works:

WHEN WE	WE ARE	THEN WE DOUBT
stay too long in what doesn't work	tolerating the intolerable.	ourselves; that is, we lose faith in our inner resources.

WHEN WE	WE ARE	THEN WE DOUBT
don't stay long enough in what can work	not tolerating what can change for the better.	the power of love; that is, we lose faith in how people can grow and how their relationships can be renewed and thrive.

The great tragedy in all this is that life can indeed pass us by. These words of Emily Dickinson refer to such a possibility: "It passes and we stay." The time to move elapses and we stay put. Of course, those five words can also refer to trusting that pain passes and we remain. It would be sad indeed if we took that truth and used it to remain inert.

In nature there is no such thing as readiness or delay. Since all is continuously evolving, all is in move-on mode. The hibernating bear is not postponing, only preparing. Likewise, a baby asleep is not escaping but growing. Time-lapse photography will show that the apparently solid oak tree outside my window is undergoing continuous changes. My tree is not standing still but flowing. Our fear of change and flow might help us understand why we would procrastinate. How relevant that our word to describe the present is *current*, which comes from a Latin word meaning "flowing." Indeed, flowing, evolving, moving on is happening all the time on our planet. In this book we will find ways to imitate nature's style of ongoing movement and growth, all and always just in time.

We will look at the combination of inner resources and the timing required to move on. We will find ways to say yes to the understated or insistent call of timing. We will look at ways to get ready, get set, and go. *Any situation we are stuck in can become a chime to awaken us from immobility.*

Here are some of the issues that might be at stake when we feel ourselves holding back from moving on:

- We may be intimidated by a partner. This partner might even threaten us with abuse if we dare leave.
- We might feel embarrassed (a form of fear) about leaving a career we worked so hard to be in.
- We might be stymied by the fear of what people will think of us for making such a choice.
- We might fear that we will have nowhere to go or wind up no better off than we are now.

- We might be afraid of how guilty we will feel after we leave.
- We might fear disappointing those in our circle of love or scandalizing those who look up to us.

As we see, one side of the coin is that we stay too long. The other side is that we leave too soon. We will look into what it takes to stay in a relationship or circumstance that *can* work out, that has more to offer us. We shall see how and when staying is valuable. Some of us sit still too long; some of us run off too soon. We want to look at the hesitations and complications that underlie our hightailing it out of a partnership or project when staying put could make it work optimally.

- We might, for instance, be caught in a fear of or refusal to enter into a commitment.
- We hold back from putting our heart and soul into a relationship, a membership, a career, a spiritual program.
- We want to keep our options open, remain carefree, reserving our ability to leave whenever we please. This can be a form of freedom, but it might also be an unwillingness to persevere, to do what it takes to make a go of something, to see something through to an end that is good for us. An example is a commitment to parenting, which entails staying at least the eighteen years responsible parenting requires.
- With regard to a relationship, we might have a fear of being fully seen, known, or held.
- We might fear allowing ourselves to be as vulnerable as is required for intimacy to flourish and then deepen. Indeed, the very word *intimacy* comes from the Latin for "deep."
- We notice that being with someone over the years will require opening ourselves at a deep level, more than we now feel ready for.
- We notice how a partner gets to know us all the way to bottom. We have kept so much hidden, but here it is out in the light. That can make us run the other way.

We can see all this without judgment against ourselves. It is indeed scary for any of us to be truly committed or fully vulnerable. But overcoming those terrors helps us grow into the full stature of humanness. We can come to see the prospect of such an enterprise with excitement rather than fear. We can look at our avoidance with self-compassion and engage in practices to free ourselves from our chill and restricting qualms.

Our work together in this book will, of course, be more about inquiry than certitude—there are too many mysteries here to promise that. But surrender to mystery is just where a journey for heroes like us best begins. We will blend psychological insight with spiritual wisdom from a variety of traditions. Then we will know that our journey to wholeness is always and already whole—as are we.

> Did you ever get the feeling that you wanted to go,
> But still had the feeling that you wanted to stay?
> —Jimmy Durante

ONE

What Makes It So Difficult to Go

All experience has shown that mankind are more disposed to suffer, while evils are sufferable, than to right themselves by abolishing the forms to which they are accustomed. But ... it is their right, it is their duty, to throw off such government, and to provide new guards for their future security.
—U.S. Declaration of Independence

STAYING TOO LONG in what doesn't work is ultimately a form of pain. An alternative path is to change conditions for the better or to exit what does not yield to improvement. Yet that's not so easy for most of us. We might, instead, linger in inadequate or untenable situations—"disposed to suffer." We might become "accustomed" to pain and stay stuck in it.

There are many reasons we might remain in an idling mode, or why we make do:

- We might be caught in delusions, false beliefs, wishful thinking.
- We might be stymied by a fear of change.
- We might believe that life is about enduring rather than enjoying.
- We might feel *compelled* to keep trying.
- We might keep our hopes up when they have led us nowhere and for too long.

A central teaching in Buddhism is the impermanent nature of things and how we cause our own suffering when we cling to what is passing. Fixation and stuckness oppose this teaching. We are imagining instead that our present situation can or *has* to go on forever. We believe in permanence, and we act as if it were real. Indeed, our fear of change is an avoidance of bedrock reality, since change is a daily given of life. When we fear making a change, we fear evolving. This is fearing the very purpose of change: to help us grow.

We might also be denying Buddha's teaching that happiness is a legitimate life goal. Instead, we cling to the unhappy but familiar status quo, a grasping that leads to suffering. To stay stuck in what goes nowhere is both denying our right to happiness and holding on to what cancels it. Sadly, we become our own gravediggers.

Here are some ways to know our situation is not working:

In an intimate relationship:

- We are deadlocked in dysfunction, and we tolerate it.
- There is no lively energy left: all has become stale and flat.
- There is neither comfort nor challenge.
- Each partner has gone in a different direction.
- One or both of us are addicts.
- Our feelings and needs don't matter nor are they fulfilled.
- Trust is gone.
- Sex is nonexistent or rare.
- All is at a standstill except ongoing resentment.
- In our daily round there are more snarls than smiles.
- We have become nothing more than roommates.

As adults relating to our family of origin:

- We are being met continually by judgment, criticism, rejection.
- Our family is emotionally needy and not making a change for the better.

- Our family members demand and have taken priority in our life choices.
- We have been given a prescribed role and are expected to stay in it. (We might also put ourselves in a role and stay in it.)
- They—or even we—believe we have no right to a life of our own.

Our friendships:

- We no longer trust one another with our deepest feelings and revelations.
- Our interactions feel competitive rather than nurturant.
- We no longer have much in common.
- One of us has become more of a therapist than a friend.
- We have been betrayed, and the other person does not take responsibility for the break in trust.
- We are both content with rare or no contact.

At our job:

- We have no future, no chance of promotion, no upside potential, only dead-end work with no opportunity for advancement.
- The workspace is competitive rather than cooperative.
- There is a lack of equitable or respectful management.
- Our skill set is not being put to use.
- Training to upgrade our skills is lacking.
- Our salary is not fair.
- We cannot trust management or peers.
- We are working (too) hard when we no longer need to do so.

Our religion:

- It is restrictive and inhibitory.
- The beliefs are not ones an adult can adhere to.

- The morality is fear- or shame-based.
- There is a lack of social consciousness.
- There is a contempt for science and a restriction against the full range of legitimate human choices.
- The only legitimate sexual orientation or social style is the mainstream one.
- The religious authorities rule and can't be questioned.
- Their biases do not reflect or support our integrity of conscience.

Our group memberships:

- We have lost interest in or commitment to the mission of the organization.
- The group or political party is no longer faithful to its own principles.
- Our interest in the group's projects has diminished significantly.
- The program no longer challenges us. We have outgrown it.

Our break from any of these predicaments will usually take a readiness based on timing. However, if there is abuse happening in any of these connections, timing no longer matters—our assignment is to leave as soon as possible for safety's sake.

Letting go is always meant to be followed by going on. Both of these are challenging for any of us. How exasperating that we would fear the two requirements of the journey we are here to undertake. Nonetheless, our self-compassion about this or any fear is a crucial step toward healthy change.

Emily Dickinson, in her poem "'Tis not that dying hurts us so," uses an analogy of two kinds of birds in the world of the four seasons. Some birds stay through the cold winter begging crumbs from reluctant farmers who, like them, are "sticking it out." On the other hand, some birds wisely migrate *before* the frosts are due. Birds act in accord with instinct. The poet compares what happens with the stay-home birds to the human *choice* not to fly off to better shores when life gets frosty. She laments that "we are the birds that stay"—a title I considered for this book.

What makes us bide our time in a limbo so nippy? The word *limbo* in Latin refers to an edge. We loiter at the edge rather than cross it into pastures new. What keeps us tied to the as-it-is? Why would we remain on a path that has shown itself to be nothing more than a dead end? Why do we hang out with indecision, inaction, passivity? It might simply be that we are slow learners. In the sections that follow we find other, more complex explanations—and exits too.

The psyche seeks balance—a combination of opposites rather than staying put in an extreme. The transcendent function of the psyche finds the midpoint, a third option between the two. This happens when the time is right—that is, in synchronicity. For example, Goldilocks leaves home, undertakes her journey, on the very morning that the three bears prepare their porridge and leave their house empty. She could not have gone earlier or later if she were to learn what she was ready to learn. Goldilocks went when the timing was just right, or synchronous. She found the first bowl too hot, the second too cold. Thus, the extremes served a purpose, as they can for any of us. They guided Goldilocks to the balance point between the extremes, the transcendent third. Goldilocks moved from one unsatisfactory bowl to the next in a matter of seconds. It may take us ten or twenty years to make our move. But it's never too late to find what's "just right."

DEFICIENCY	JUST RIGHT	EXCESS
Not enough: We may be stuck here.	Where we belong	Too much: We may be stuck here.

WHEN WE AREN'T READY
TO KNOW OR NAME

> O crescent moon,
> I too am hiding
> So much of me.

In Genesis, chapter 9, Noah in his tent is so drunk he has thrown off all his clothes. His son Ham knows his father's condition. He stands guard outside the tent lest others find out about it. Ham asks his two brothers to go in and deal with the problem. Shem and Japheth then walk in but backward so as not to see Noah in his woebegone state. They throw a cloth over their father to cover up his nakedness. This story shows how denial works in alcoholism. Denial may work in these same ways with respect to our topics:

- We don't look directly at the problem because we are afraid to see its extent.
- We keep it all in the family.
- We ask others to deal with the problem for us.
- We make an inroad but still don't look directly at the situation.
- We engage in a cover-up and take that to be sufficient.
- We are afraid to know the real nature of our relationship to someone.

Readiness refers both to knowing and to acting. The path to any action begins with realizing what is really going on: Ham's situation. But the next step is taking effective action to help their father toward a program of recovery. None of the three brothers could go that far. And their half measures avail nothing if healing is ever to happen.

Using a positive example, we have to know we are in good enough shape before we can run a marathon. We have to feel we are cut out for intimate relating before we can look for a successful partnership. But it may not be that simple. There is such a thing as not knowing yet because the time to know has not come yet. For instance, it may take time to realize we are introverts. Only then can we plan our lifestyle—and partnership—accordingly. "The time to know" and "take time" lead us to an essential element of our topic: timing.

Audre Lorde in *Sister Outsider*, asked: "How much of this truth can I bear to see and still live unblinded . . . ?" She reminds us there is also a not knowing because it is unsafe to know—even our own deepest needs, values, and wishes. In this instance, timing kicks in when safety is assured or when safety has ceased to matter because we have become so courageous.

The fear of knowing our own truth or the truth about a relationship is sometimes concealed under other fears. A mother has difficulty relating to her adult son. She is afraid to put the cards on the table and ask him to join her in improving their relationship. She knows she will then hear what to him are old as yet unspoken resentments. The mother knows she will have to confront her own regrets about his childhood with her. What holds her back is her fear that the conversation might expose his rejection and her own inadequacy. But both fears come down to the one fear of knowing the full truth about the woeful state of their relationship. Most of us have struck bargains with family members, workmates, partners: "If I don't rock the boat by delving in, we won't ever sink." This is ultimately admitting, though not yet fully comprehended, that the capsizing has already happened.

The real name of a fear like this may be dread of having the truth come out. If it does, it will trigger us more than the keep-it-up-in-the-air style we have both settled into. And, the bottom-line, ultimate reason for our fear has no name at all. It is lodged in experiences from the distant past, too far away to see directly, too hidden in the shuffle of memories to have a name.

Why do we refuse to know the reality or truth of our life predicament? What makes us turn our full gaze away from the portrait of our pain? Sometimes, it is not deliberate: We just don't realize or even notice we are unhappy because we have become so used to our unhappiness. We have become so accustomed to our suffering that it is simply wallpaper in our psyches and bodies. In a relationship situation we may have become used to being wounded by friendly fire. It may even have become soothing in some inexplicable way. We sit mute and unaware on the silent shore of Lethe, the murky river of forgetfulness.

An exacting taboo might have been imposed upon us since early life. Knowing who we really were was off-limits; we were defined only in accord with our parents' or other authority figures' strict and limited depiction of us. Knowing our needs was prohibited; we were *told* our needs. We might even have been told they were adequately satisfied when, deep down, we knew otherwise. Knowing our gifts and talents might have led to a frown from parents who had other plans for our future. In our household, knowing or naming our ideas, our beliefs, our gender, our sexual orientation, our bodily sensations, our true passions might have been perilous. If they were not mainstream, we were in danger of becoming outcasts, put on the fast train to isolation, or even to hellfire.

Knowing we had a dark side was certainly hazardous in a family in which being a "good" boy or girl was the only safe option. Knowing or showing we were different might have been perilous in a family or in any group that insisted on uniformity. In childhood, before we had our full quiver of personal powers, we could only know what the family thought it was safe for us to know, only feel what would be safe for us to feel, only choose what was safe to choose. Thus, we were held up on the path to knowing our unique identity, feeling our feelings, and acting in accord with them. We know ourselves through our own deepest feelings, needs, values, wishes, and longings. If it was only safe in our childhood home to have the ones our caretakers approved of, how can we know ourselves now? All this restriction stunts our growth toward readiness for any scary move. Indeed, all moves become scary.

Childhood taboos, as well as a lack of self-knowledge, can carry over into adult life. We might still not know ourselves or our needs—closely related—and not even realize we don't know. We might not recognize that our life situation is unacceptable to us. Perhaps choosing a book like this was a sign that something was ready to be explored. The trail into that recognition is fearlessly knowing ourselves all the way to the bottom, recognizing what part of the woods we are standing in at the moment. So what chance do we have for the journey into forests a lifetime is meant to explore?

In the New Testament, St. Philip asks a passerby who is reading if he understands the text. The reply is in Acts 8:31: "How can I know unless someone show me?" Sometimes our knowing depends on the voice of someone else. Sometimes knowing ourselves hangs on a word from a person who understands us better than we understand ourselves. We may find out what we are really about from the wise friend or guide. This is the one who knows us not judgmentally but supportively. Then there is no fear in us about self-discovery or self-revelation. We become able to see ourselves through eyes that see better than we can.

Let's look at this in reverse. Let's say we are the ones who know— but can't help our friend know, only trust he will find out on his own. I will use a personal example. My home is adjacent to a golf course. Today I saw a bag of clubs fall off the back of a player's golf cart as he was riding it away. I had no time to warn him or catch up with him, but I was sure that he would notice it soon enough. Thus, I knew he would know in his own time but could not help him know in my time. All I could do was watch out for his golf bag. I recognized this whole experience as a metaphor about timing. Sometimes we know people's truth before they do. Yet we have to wait for them to realize on their own.

We may see and explain exactly how a family member or friend's situation is unmanageable although options are many. Unfortunately, our words can reach only the prefrontal cortex, the reasoning, assessing center of this person's brain. Staying stuck has its origins in the limbic system where emotions are lodged, or even in the amygdala where traumas are trapped. Words don't reach that far in. The timing is not ours to influence. Likewise, all the other elements of immobility speak more loudly than you ever can. We speak cortically, but fears are limbic—two very different languages. We can only stay present in a witnessing, hoping way. In this witnessing style we are showing love since we are accepting without blaming, allowing without interfering.

Sometimes admonitions we heard in childhood obscure the revelation of the true story about ourselves and our predicament: "Stick it out, see it through, be the little engine that could, shut up and take it, never be a quitter, don't give up no matter what." Tenacity and perseverance are certainly virtues, but they can also be foils to keep us stuck. Yet we don't need to blame ourselves, for sometimes—or even often—being in the dark about our life and predicament. We understand that it will be hard to know what action to take when we are not ready to take it. This is how *knowing* and *doing* rely on matching timing with readiness. We can only know the necessity of going when we are ready to go. The knowing is receptivity, the openness that may usher us to readiness.

Not knowing includes not allowing ourselves to feel the full impact of events and quandaries. Indeed, we only allow ourselves to know the meaning of our situation in proportion to our resources to handle it. For instance, abuse may put us at an impasse. We don't doubt our ability to tolerate what is happening, but we are doubting our ability to make a change. In that predicament we no longer even see that a change is possible. In what follows we shall explore some of the feelings and circumstances that obscure our vision of the path and our chance to walk it to new vistas.

The word *olim* in Latin has three meanings. When it refers to the past, it means "formerly." When it refers to the present, it means "for a while now." When it refers to the future, it means "hereafter." What if the word *timing* could be used the same way? In that instance, knowing our timing would embrace what has happened formerly, what has been happening for a while, and what might happen in the future. Quite a challenge indeed.

One final word regarding not knowing: willful ignorance is the unfortunate option some people choose. Our choice has to change to willful knowing in order for any alteration or real satisfaction to be possible. Here are two obvious or subtle forms of keeping ourselves in the dark and thereby hobbled for life's journey:

- We are misreading and misled. We are hearing taps in a relationship or career, but we believe we are hearing reveille. We don't want to hearken to the message being sent to us so loudly and clearly. We don't want to see the full picture. We don't want to know what might require a follow-up action, especially the actions of going, of changing, or of ending.
- We are hoping that the negative situation will alter on its own or that the other person's behavior will soon change for the better.

But *the only hope worthy of the name is the hope that is activated by evidence of change*. True hope is based on what we see, not what we wish for while we are denying reality. Hope, wishful thinking, and dogged denial are the same sometimes. But hope is none of these when we are focused on and loyal to what is—as it is—with no future plan in motion.

The first step toward moving out of what hurts us is knowing we are hurting, naming it as hurt, unveiling the wound that has remained hidden for so long. Our vocabulary changes then from "I have to stay put" to "Get me out of here." But that impulse toward freedom can only begin with the will to know. Indeed, Rumpelstiltskin won't let us be until we name him in no uncertain terms.

[When individuation happens,] the situation has thrown off the conventional husk and developed into a stark encounter with reality, with no false veils or adornments of any kind.
—Carl Jung, *The Psychology of the Transference*

OUR FEARS MAY BE BULLYING US

Fear is the primary reason we stay stuck. We might be afraid of what life will be like when we leave where we are and venture into something new. Our fears may be of change, of the future, of the new, of leaving the present and the familiar. But there is more to this fear. It may also be fear that we won't *survive* if we are out there on our own. We doubt the fiber of our own autonomy, a subject we will explore in chapter 3. A relationship or affiliation may be a cozy refuge from a world we don't believe we can navigate on our own.

Let's begin by noticing that every fear we have is about not being in control of what may happen, a dread of powerlessness, an unease about surprise. We are doubting our inner resources. We may be so manipulated by fear that we even believe being in control is one and the same as being safe. Our entire sense of self then depends on how much in control we are in all areas of life. We don't believe we can survive by letting the chips fall where they may; we have to be in charge of how they land, every time. We might also believe it will be frightening to step over the threshold of the familiar, leaving "the devil we know" to meet "the devil we don't know." The name of that demon is not Lucifer; it is "Letting Go of Control."

When we imagine that our fulcrum of stability is control, we are automatically denying reality. We can be so intent on controlling a partner, for instance, that we don't notice the reality of how unhappy we are in the relationship. A given of life is that no one can maintain full control in any area. The carefully constructed "all under control" life at home or work is a house of cards. The only reliable fulcrum on which a life can be poised is surrender to facts, including the fact that we are staying too long in what doesn't work.

All forms of fear may turn us into disbelievers in our capacity to go on, skeptical we can pull off a change, convinced we should put it off indefinitely. Fear dictates to us that we have to wait for more information, for a rescuer, for someone else to make the first move, such as a partner in a dead-end relationship. We hang back, freeze up, put things on hold, postpone, discard opportunities in favor of procrastination. We may stall, hesitate on the brink, vacillate about what our decision should be, waver about a choice we have approved of mentally. We might have come to see ourselves as frightened children who can't possibly cross the rickety bridge from what is to what can be. In fact, we are sure there is no "what can be." We have sat so long in the ashes of self-discarding that we can't access our phoenix-soul. We can't see the new blossoms budding in any vacant lot.

Sometimes our fear of going has an ironic twist. We believe staying put is *necessary* because we would not make it alone. We are not in touch with our inner resources; we feel more like lost souls than captains of our destiny. We imagine we will be nobody if we are not defined by others or an institution. We rely on what has been, though it does not nurture us, but has only kept us safe from our terror about launching. A relationship, group, political organization, or cult may pander to that fear and exploit it.

Our fear of going might be based on timidity, on an inner realization, accurate or not, that we can't make it on our own. We *need* a structure around us, be it a relationship or a religion or any affiliation that tells us what to think and how to act. We can't imagine designing all that on our own. Such a misapprehension can hearken back to childhood when life in our family home was chaotic indeed. We felt we were incapable of surviving in it, but we could not leave. So we attached ourselves to something that gave us a sense of order and safety. Our family life—or an adult situation recently—may have destabilized us, cast us into insecurity, and we could not self-stabilize and get back on track. We had nothing to turn to, no way of framing our experience, no way of understanding it or settling it.

It may have been a religious organization or spiritual community that gave us a framework, a way of making sense of the world and ourselves. The price we paid was our own independence, what we feared anyway. All we had to do was follow the party line, embrace beliefs without question, abide by the rules, honor authority. We misinterpreted safety and security as requiring a relinquishing of autonomy. We stayed in what was the *equivalent* of a holding, nurturing environment—one, however, that did not bless and keep our identity but canceled it order to clone us. We now had something reliable to hold on to in a whirlpool world. We hung on because that felt like loyalty to what had saved us. All this indeed worked, but only because we were not yet able to act, think, or live on our own. It was not fully about a price we had to pay; it was the only game in town that we could trust.

Our fear-driven options were absolute: isolation or connection, chaos or obedience. No one was forcing us; we were glad to have found what we believed we needed for our survival. Thus, what someone might have called fear of going was to us need fulfillment. We needed safety for survival, and we found it. Obedience was now felicitously equated with security. We had no ground, but now we were grounded—albeit in both senses.

Someday we may build inner resources, gain a sense of personal autonomy, and construct our own framework of suitable beliefs, attitudes, and behaviors. Then we have options, for instance, regarding a religious affiliation: We can join a new religion or group, one that fosters freedom. We can leave altogether. We can appreciate that our affiliation has served a purpose but is no longer applicable. We can then put the institution to one side while remaining in a home-base community of faith, keeping what was positive while no longer having to live under any thumb. Or we can launch out on our own, while still taking advantage of resources around us. They will, of course, be the ones that respect, cherish, and advance our freedom. No one of these choices is necessarily better than the others. Otherwise we are back in the Lilliputian land of absolutes where Gulliver's travels come to an abrupt halt.

WE BELIEVE WE ARE HERE TO ENDURE
RATHER THAN TO BE HAPPY

Many of us were taught that the important thing in life is to endure pain. That fiction can become the governing principle of our choices for the rest of our life. We believe we have no other option, that we don't deserve happiness. We believe we are strong because we are adept at tolerating a painful situation. We may tell ourselves it is "pain for gain," yet we don't give it up when no gain comes our way. We choose enduring over advancing—ultimately a masochistic style.

No situation or relationship produces happiness every minute. When a low dividend of happiness comes our way, we can *temporarily* reconcile ourselves to it. But at the same time, we remain on target when we keep seeking a higher dividend anyway. The words *at the same time* give us a clue to the difference between a healthy tolerance of pain and an unhealthy enduring of pain. Our capacity to tolerate *due pain* is a stepping-stone to strengthening ourselves, increasing our inner resources. For example, we endure physical pain after an accident while *at the same time* being faithful to a physical therapy program. In spiritual consciousness, this protocol also leads to compassion for those who suffer as we do. We look through our own wounds and see the wounds of others, perhaps unnoticed before. Our seeing leads to compassionate action, as the Good Samaritan saw and then acted on what he saw.

We recall the familiar prayer about having the serenity to accept what can't be changed but *at the same time* having the courage to change what can be changed. We stay in a job, relationship, affiliation long enough to work out that combination. When it can't happen, we move on. Here is an example: We endure a lack of need fulfillment in a relationship, accept what isn't changing. We commit ourselves to pursuing couple's therapy and any other resources, attempting to make a change. We exit the relationship when the issue can't be changed even with state-of-the-art means, such as self-help techniques or therapy.

Therapy can offer two wonderful options: we find out our own truth and we gain the courage to act on that truth. Direct experience of our own reality is an antidote to self-deception. Taking action based on the reality of ourselves and our life situation is an antidote to inertia. Sometimes the "work" is not action, only witnessing mindfully until we are moved to shift our focus to what comes next. Yes, sometimes we do have to *wait* to be moved.

We might think it is indisputable that we are here to endure pain, so we numb ourselves to the natural built-in gauge that tells us when it has become too much. We lose our sense of boundaries—especially when we have been taught we are here not to succeed but to exceed. Believing we always *have to* be more than what we are is a form of pain. We might even lose our sense of who is worthy of our trust because we have bought into the attitude that we are here to suffer or be hurt, as Job 13:15 says: "Though he slay me yet will I trust him."

In the quotation at the beginning of this chapter from the Declaration of Independence, Thomas Jefferson says that we "are more disposed to suffer, *while evils are sufferable.*" Do we remain in pain because we *can*? "As long as I have the ability to tolerate this, it must be right to stay in it." We fail to see that such a capacity is not the equivalent of wise choice. We cancel our chances at happiness when we are driven by such a mentality. Direction has overtaken discernment.

We may become quite adroit at rationalizing. We tell ourselves that enduring builds character. We deny that in some instances enduring is not in our best interest. Mitt Romney, in a speech in February 2020 regarding his voting in favor of Donald Trump's impeachment, gave us an insight into why we stay stuck through rationalization: "I have found, in business in particular but also in politics, that when something is in your personal best interests, the ability of the mind to rationalize that that's the right thing is really quite extraordinary. . . . I have seen it in others, and I have seen it in myself."

The word *endure* comes from a Latin word meaning "harden." The same Latin root gives us the word *durance*, which means "imprisonment, loss of freedom." We harden ourselves against change—and the libera-tion it will bring. Enduring is anti-evolutionary. Instead of evolving, we are stopping the show—that is, keeping things as they are even until the final curtain. We are invested in keeping everything the same—a danger-ous definition of success. For beings born to journey success can't mean permanent toleration of what is. It has to mean stepping into what can be with audacity and alacrity. The word *alacrity* means "cheerful, lively, and prompt readiness"—what a wonderful motto!

Many of us learned to value the enduring of pain in our religious upbringing. It is characteristic of the Protestant ethic, for instance, that hard work is a supreme value. In some religious traditions, suffering is the surest portal into heaven. We note the irony: happiness is a legiti-mate goal after all but only in an afterlife.

Our statement when we endure unhappiness may be: "I am here to give too much." We may have learned it was selfish to have healthy boundaries. We see an example of this attitude in a Catholic prayer composed by St. Ignatius of Loyola:

Lord, teach me to be generous.
Teach me to serve as you deserve,
to give and not to count the cost,
to fight and not to heed the wounds,
to toil and not to seek for rest,
to labor and not to ask for any reward,
save that of knowing that I am doing your holy will.

Yet, it is not healthy to forgo reciprocation entirely or to disregard boundaries that maintain our health and sanity. The prayer asks that we pay no attention to our wounds rather than to notice them and then adjust our level of giving to a reasonable level. It does not acknowledge our need for rest, which we say God gladly did on the Sabbath in the Bible story of creation. Here is a less poetic version of the prayer that safeguards our psychological health, which we all need to have in place if we are ever to fulfill our calling to growth and service. A calling is to something to live for, something bigger than just living. That will take upkeep of our body-mind, the only instrument we have to be healthy and holy:

Lord, teach me to be generous,
to give without stint all that is appropriate to give,
to fight and take time to heal my—and others'—wounds,
to toil and enjoy periods of rest,
to labor and appreciate a reward without demanding one.
This balance of giving and self-caring is how I know that I am
doing your holy will that I be whole and wholesome.

This promotes an alternative to self-negating endurance. Instead we are choosing balance and happiness. We recall John Milton's statement that "God and Nature bid the same." In mature religious consciousness, the divine will is not meant to contradict the human nature it designed.

Many religious teachings say that pain is a path to redemption. It can indeed be that. For instance, we can feel a call to make changes in ourselves or in our society. Then we fight with all our might on a path, however agonizing, as Martin Luther King Jr. did. He endured anguish in order to move us all into a new way of being human toward ourselves and others. He used pain to keep moving on—while maintaining a spirit of joy and hope. But that is different from using toleration of pain to stay put. We are not then becoming more human; we are not emancipating ourselves and others. We are only sitting in the bleachers watching others move from base to base rather than joining the game that takes us around the diamond essence.

WE FIND WAYS TO STAY WHILE DISTANCING

We sometimes stay in a relationship or situation because we have found a way to make it manageable. We come up with an accommodation and then become used to it. For instance, in a marriage we may be living as roommates with no intimacy, but it is OK with both of us. We have found a way to be together and distant simultaneously. We imagine the détente *is* working, but in reality our relationship has become inert and we are going nowhere. Brief periods of inertness can be useful in relationships when they are bridges to new chapters.

There are many ways we make relationships manageable—let's look at two ways this might happen: finding a distraction or staying mainly to get revenge. In both we see that we are staying put, but it is actually a distancing. The distraction makes for shelter against intimacy. The revenge makes for canceling it altogether. Both are ultimately about staying in what still doesn't work and using means that aren't in anyone's best interests.

Finding and Using a Distraction

Partners in a relationship that has lost its spark may find an outside something or someone that makes an uneasy predicament endurable for both of them. A third presence in the relationship compensates for what is missing or makes tolerable what has become intolerable. This third stands between the partners so they don't have to look at one another directly. The third can be a concern, a person, an infidelity, an excessive focus on children, critical financial issues, pets, money, illness, addiction, resentments, or any problem or condition that just doesn't go away. The third element serves as a focus that distracts the partners from seeing what is actually happening in the relationship, looking honestly at what is missing, and looking directly at one another and all their woes.

In a relationship, an example of the third that extends a negative status quo can be the person with whom a partner is having an affair. This third may serve as a pointer to what is happening, the voice that proclaims the emperor has no clothes. The new lover can help one or both partners understand what has been or is missing in the relationship. Indeed, a lover might be *upholding* an unsatisfying marriage, helping both spouses tolerate what has become empty. The new person may be helping both of them stay too long in what doesn't work. When the supporting prop—the affair—ends, the deficiency of the long-standing marriage becomes evident. Now the spouses can taste their own unsavory truth and proceed accordingly, either to therapy or to separate tables. The one between them showed them there was nothing between them! Not every affair has this meaning, but any affair reveals something about the state of the original relationship. An affair is not a wholesome thoroughfare to the truth about a failing bond, but sometimes it works in that way.

Sometimes the "between" is the only foundation of a house of cards, and they blessedly collapse at last. This applies to any situation or association that has been sustained by what is now no longer happening: If our attachment to a career was based on pleasing a spouse or parent, then when they are gone so is our connection to it. When our religious affiliation is based on pleasing our parents and grandparents, our subscription fades fast when they have expired. If our religion is tied to the national origin of our family, we may believe that forsaking it would be an act of disloyalty. Thus, we don't break ranks though we no longer believe in the teachings or follow the directives. We feel secure as part of a group that reflects our history, that offers rituals the whole family celebrates. We stay for that sense of belonging, a source of security. We are thus close to it and distant from it at the same time.

Staying Long Enough to Get Revenge

One can fall in love and still hate.
—Fyodor Dostoyevsky

We can't overlook a sinister motivation to stay put in a relationship at home or work. It might be so toxic that one or both people stay only so that they can keep getting back at one another for past hurts. This can certainly happen at a job or in an affiliation we have come to dislike or in which we feel we have been disrespected. Usually the revenge motive is based on a long-term resentment or a list of resentments. Maladaptive motivations can keep people together for years. They can also keep people in a job or association even though everyone winds up suffering.

In a toxic relationship or association we may feel hatred arising in us toward others. Hate has four deadly ingredients: intense hostility, ill-will, an intent to harm or wish that harm would happen, and an insatiable need for revenge. Hate has its origin in fear, rage, or injury. It can also be one of the results of trauma. A victim will often hold hate against a perpetrator until full healing and letting go can happen. Those who abused us scared us. The ego can't tolerate being intimidated. We will, consciously or unconsciously, hate and be enraged at those who scare us.

We may also hold anger or hate against those we have given our power to. If a woman is needy for a man in order to feel whole, she may also hold hostility toward men. If a man fears upsetting women because he needs them to feel whole, he may also be angry at women, even unbeknownst to himself. Perhaps misogyny is ultimately fear of women rather than just hate. Our path out of hate has to pass first through the door of freedom from fear. The key to that door is letting go of aggression in favor of love, a long and winding road indeed. This is where loving-kindness practice is essential for personal and spiritual growth. It smooths the road to real wholeness.

Within relationships at home or work we might engage in aggressive behavior openly or passively. Aggression is open when we are directly abusive. It is passive when we do or fail to do what honors the ground rules of the relationship. It can also be shown by the silent treatment or other exasperating words or behaviors meant to frustrate someone.

Our resentment, expressed as aggression, is ultimately an avoidance of grief about how we are not getting what we believe is coming to us. Indeed, any hurt we sustain in a relationship evokes sadness in us. In a less healthy response we may immediately cover or avoid that grief reaction with retaliatory rage. That is not anger; it is abuse. When, instead, we open to our grief, we express nonviolent anger as part of it. We are admitting our sadness and vulnerability rather than hiding it. Thus our feeling hurt can lead to more closeness between ourselves and the other. In revenge hurt leads to division, sometimes for a lifetime. With a tear and a healthy "ouch!" we have a chance at connecting.

A spiritual practice can also make a difference. I paraphrase a teaching from the Buddhist *Majjhima Nikaya Sutra*: "We will not be ungrounded by what others do. We will not use hurtful words. We will stay centered in compassion, caring for others' well-being, with a heart of loving-kindness, and with no hate."

Here is a story relevant to our topic. I was giving a workshop at a Buddhist retreat center on my book *How to Be an Adult in Relationships*. One-third of the audience was made up of couples. We were on the topic of retribution as a toxic style in relationships. I had mentioned that I was seeing the retaliation style in many counseling sessions with couples. I was ending my comments with this: "How can intimacy be real when we still engage in revenge? How can hurting back when we are hurt help us love more?" Then, out of nowhere, without having planned to say it beforehand, I heard myself saying: "What if, at breakfast tomorrow morning, you were to tell your partner that you have made a decision: 'No matter what you may do to upset me from here on in, I will never resort to revenge as my response. And I don't ask you to make the same commitment.' You say this with no need for a reply." There were over 150 people in the room, but there was total silence after I said this. The participants were staring at me. Suddenly I realized that I had put them on the spot. If at breakfast they did *not* say what I suggested, were they, in effect, declaring that they did indeed intend to retaliate? It was an uncomfortable moment. I see now I was pushing too hard. In addition, I was not allowing for individual timing, which can reach beyond breakfast. It can take quite a while to decide to forgo vengeance in our relationships or even see the value of such a practice. Most of us were brought up with the belief that we should get back at people. (In my Italian upbringing, revenge was not only legitimate; it was required—as the *Godfather* films reminded me.)

Now I rephrase it all again to you, reader—as a prompt not a push: Ask yourself what it will take to let go of retaliating if you have been doing so. Ask yourself if you want to keep using revenge as a go-to when you are treated unfairly or when your feelings are hurt. Ask if vengeance fits your spiritual practices, especially loving-kindness. What will it take no longer to seek reprisals in your interactions? Wait till you truly want to stop exacting retribution in favor of exploring reconciliation. Then, or anytime, consider the route of committing to this spiritual practice of grief with healthy anger: being sad, saying "ouch!" and then opening a dialogue, asking for amends, letting go with love and without resentment. You now have more creative and more love-building options. What happened to me when I made my vow to Buddha to let go of revenge was simple: I liked myself more. The timing for my vow was not based on any thought or plan. It arose from an inner readiness, appearing from beyond the precincts of my mind, a grace indeed.

> The anger, the resentment, the bitterness, the desire for recrimination against people you believe have wronged you: they harden the heart, deaden the spirit, and lead to self-inflicted wounds.
> —Bill Clinton, talk at Union Chapel, Oak Bluffs,
>   Massachusetts, 1998

> One act of retaliation burns down a whole forest of merit.
> —Dhammapada

WE ARE UNDER THE SPELL OF CHILDHOOD

Childhood development proceeds on the basis of modeling. We learn how to be human by watching humans, especially our parents. Unfortunately, this can wind up being a negative catechism indeed.

Seeing our parents in an empty relationship might have led us to believe we deserved no better in our later relationships. In this context, *empty* means "loveless, juiceless, immobile." Each partner goes a separate way, no intimacy in the offing. Our parents' relationship could also have been a dead-end drama: constantly bringing up old resentments, being abusive toward one another, insulting, blaming, shaming—nothing resolved. We saw their flint and steel interactions and perhaps absorbed a belief that couples *are* that way. If we join this belief to the one that recommends enduring, we might add: "But all that matters is that they stuck it out." This also means perpetuating our pain is legitimate all through our lives—a veto on exiting. A hero may go through a *phase* of immobility as part of the journey. A victim is immobilized permanently, with no journey at all.

When we saw no fulfillment of needs between our parents or toward us, no joy in being together, no lively energy, how could we live on but in despair? Now it comes as no surprise to us that our own relationship is no better than theirs was. This too makes it well-nigh impossible to leave. Our imagination has been hobbled by our past. We can't imagine an alternative when we are conditioned into knowing only one. We can't trust ourselves; we lose access to grounding. Our past is dictating the style of the present. Our goal is to discard these conditioned responses in favor of free choices.

Modeling is also identifying. Our mother's immobility, like her fears, might be governing our life now. We may be living her life by feeling her fears and thinking they are our own. In this instance, separation from family, leaving home, has not fully happened. Yet we can keep finding ways in this book to see our life not as a rerun but as a premiere.

In addition to what we learned about relationships from our parental models, there were other homespun influences. The first was trauma: Some difficult experiences in childhood landed on us in a superficial way. Some hit us deep within—and there was a wide spectrum in between. An example of a superficially distressing experience, remembered as such, happened when we wanted an ice-cream cone before dinner and our parents insisted we wait till after dinner. On the other hand, traumatic experiences, such as parents starving us when we did not obey them, opens a deep long-standing wound. That trauma takes time to work on and, even then, may never arrive at full closure. Trauma has a timing all its own; we can't hurry or delay it. Let's look at some features of trauma.

Not fully knowing our pain, or becoming aware of it in layers, is part of an abuse cycle. We dissociate from recollection of an event or its extent. Trauma in childhood is nonetheless logged in our body-mind memory. When trauma happened, its full implications might have been dulled if it was not mirrored or validated by our parents. The story we tell ourselves and others is then abridged: At eight years old, Sebastian saw his father seriously assault his mother. This was a traumatic event for Sebastian, replete with feelings, meanings, bodily resonances of terror, grief, and powerlessness. Yet, on the day the trauma occurred and thereafter, neither of Sebastian's parents checked in with him about his reactions or feelings. They did not mirror them; they did not acknowledge them; they did not hold him through them. Instead, the event was never mentioned at all. Sebastian walked on the dark side of the moon all alone. What was to him a gigantic event thereby became even more unsettling and confounding. The more isolated we are in our wounding, the more lasting our trauma. We might even wonder if it really happened, a result of holding something inside unshared and uncomprehended.

When Sebastian tells his story now as an adult, it might sound like this: "I witnessed domestic violence when I was eight." He may describe it this way because he is not yet prepared to face the full scope of his experience, not yet feeling safe to do so. This is not his fault, only a matter of a for-now limited capacity, an unreadiness to let a pillaging trauma resound fully in his body-mind.

A new in-depth version will be spoken by Sebastian when a timing beyond his control ushers him to self-exploration, a path to wholeness:

"I witnessed my father go out of control and injure my mother when I was eight. I felt so many things and so much confusion. I especially remember how alone I felt in that experience. I know I have never plumbed the depths of the event or of my response to it. I want to feel it safely now, peer into its tangle of meanings, locate its vestiges buried alive in my body, detect its shaping function in my psyche, and finally accept the ultimate inconsolability and enigma of it." Sebastian has come home to himself.

We keep in mind that working on our childhood wounds does not make them go away. Rather, we courageously and creatively find a new way of holding our past traumas so that they no longer injure us but only open us. Using an archetypal metaphor, the resurrection does not make the crucifixion go away. But it profoundly changes its meaning from execution to redemption. In both instances, personal and archetypal, the transition is from mourning to morning.

Abuse can take the forms of repression of our natural instincts and being guilt-tripped. Many of us are taught in adolescence to abstain from any sexual experimentation that helps us know and enjoy our bodies. We might also have been taught it would be wrong to live with a committed partner before marriage. We might have been intimidated into believing that same-sex love was verboten. Society in recent years has helped us no longer have to hold guilt, though our family or religion may not have yet liberated themselves from those unhealthy prejudices. A healthy childhood, relationship, or circumstance grants hospitality to all that we are.

Guilt is about breaking rules, but shame is about being broken. Shame adds the sense of being damaged, permanently wounded. There are two kinds of shame: freedom-enhancing or freedom-endangering. Being ashamed to go naked in public is freedom-enhancing because it safeguards our liberty. People will look at us with disdain. The law will punish our nakedness by taking away our freedom. But not to be able to be naked with our lover inhibits our freedom. Having that shame about nakedness is freedom-endangering.

What am I ashamed to reveal?

What has to be in place for me to expand my range of self-revelation?

Do I believe people love who I am or love my portrayal of who I am?

We Couldn't Pack a Bag

Freedom from abuse rightly links with leaving. Yet no matter what the abuse in early life, we couldn't launch out on our own: We could not run away at age four or ten or even fifteen because we would not have been able to take care of ourselves on our own. We were forced to stay put—what can then become a lifelong habit. We may feel ourselves frozen in place today even when a relationship or experience has become painful.

We also keep in mind that we stayed in our house of abuse because we loved the people there. We loved the very parents who were harming us; we loved our siblings who were under the gun too. We did not want to abandon them to the abuse they would receive or were receiving. In this instance, enduring pain became heroic caring. Yet, somehow in the midst of it all, three elements dangerously came together: love, hurt, stuckness. Now in adult life that tragic triad remains in place—as do we. Love is the gift; feeling hurt is the price; stuckness is the self-negating commitment. Yet for those of us who have had to live through traumatic times, it all feels so right, this sheltering in place.

We can be released from the clenching of the past tightening around our life in the present. The bridge is mindfulness, reality-based witnessing. We may still believe we can't leave a painful situation, our old belief dictating to us now. But we can use the four-part exercise of yes to our present adult reality, seeing our present situation from a new vantage point of gratitude for our adult inner resources:

- Yes, in the past I was abused, overwhelmed, isolated, and had no resources. Conditions made me have to stay; conditions made it unsafe to go.

- None of this is true now. I can see my past but from a safe balcony in a new present. I have adult ways of handling pain. My adult self can caretake my inner child, no longer alone or immobilized.
- I am thankful for my present strengths and the supportive resources within and around me. May I keep calling on them—and appreciating them.
- And through all that has happened, I accept my story and what it has done to me. I can be this brave because, no matter what the past has done to me, it cannot interrupt this perilous precious journey into what comes next.

When Parents Know Best

Obedience may have played a major role in our familial and religious upbringing. We understand now as adults—and maybe understood then—that obedience is top-down while nurturing our growth thrives on mutual respect. We learn to think for ourselves while hearing the opinions of others. When the obedience demanded of us in childhood also came at the cost of being loved, then "love" was nothing more than reward. It was meted out only to someone submissive by someone dominating.

Authentic love is a free gift, a grace, not based on merit gained or regulations observed. This does not refer to house rules meant to keep us safe. This is blind obedience coming as the alternative to punishment. Such a style has no place in a household built on a foundation of love. There love includes *allowing* as support of our learning to self-regulate, self-police, self-preserve, self-declare, all in an atmosphere of trial and error. The trials do not result in verdicts against us. The errors are not met with shaming of us. We note also, in this context, that obedience is not an adult virtue. It now applies only to societal rules that are meant to ensure freedom and safety for all—e.g., traffic rules.

Childhood abuse by an authority figure such as a parent may still be disempowering us in the present. Trauma is not all about the slaps Dad dealt us. The main trauma was in the humiliation and powerlessness we felt while they were being inflicted. The trauma was in the betrayal we felt when the one who was deputed to love us hurt us. The vestiges of being shamed and humiliated can make us now lose our power to duck, to defend ourselves, to speak up and say: "No more of that!" We are terrified to speak truth to power. We are too afraid to defend ourselves. We keep obeying bullies. An even more dangerous reaction to shame is becoming the bully, aggressive and vengeful.

Oppression by society is the same disempowering abuse that can hold us back from what the Founding *Fathers* coaxed us to do: "But . . . it is their right, it is their duty, to throw off such government, and to provide new guards for their future security." This advises: "Don't tread on me," not "Take it on the chin." We won't forget, of course, that those same wise fathers often failed to extend their sense of freedom to others, particularly the nonwhite population of our country.

When the ones who hurt us seemed to love us and we loved them, we were also conditioned into believing that love makes the inflicting of pain *legitimate*: "The one who loves me is allowed to hurt me." (What a twist on allowing as a form of loving.) Thus, a major reason that some of us can't leave what doesn't work is that we are still being stymied by this childhood delusion. We *choose* to stay put now because we *had* to stay put then. What an anachronism to be ensnared in. How much self-compassion do we deserve for not easily extricating ourselves from this clash of vying feelings.

Those of us who were brought up under a crucifix might have come to believe in the *divine* legitimacy of parental violence. We saw the son of God nailed to the cross in accord with his father's will. We were taught that was not only allowed but even necessary for our own redemption. In the crucifix we see the ancient patriarchal privilege: this is what a father is allowed to do to his son/child. Our salvation could only happen because a son was tortured and killed. We were advised that we too were called to suffer, our only access to a passport through the pearly gates. Or maybe we even learned, in a not so conscious but certainly lasting way, that loving a parent included letting ourselves be hurt. This can apply to any patriarchal family or society.

A Personal Note

Looking into a present feeling or experience can also show us something, as yet unnamed, from our past and depict what happened to us. After all, memories that dared not give their full names surely never let us go. I live in California, and we have our own beautiful flora here. But occasionally, I find a flower here that blooms in Connecticut, where I spent my childhood. I lean over to smell the rare lilac or the rambler rose. Suddenly I feel a deep depression, a sinking in the pit of my stomach. That same olfactory memory hits me every time. I know I am feeling exactly what I must have felt long ago in childhood. The sensation then was not evinced by flowers. It was all-covering wallpaper in the daily scenario of home. In those days, I had no vocabulary for how I felt. Nor was there anyone to blame. It was just like that: no recollection of entry, no exit either, something dun, a pall over my spirit, no alternative—what I now know to be childhood depression. I still can't say I recall that mood happening in me, but the lilacs tell me otherwise, and they, like my body, never lie.

Finally, we remind ourselves not to be discouraged as we look back at childhood. No matter how we have been treated in our past, no matter what is happening to us now, no matter what may come our way in future days, our capacity to love can never go away or even wane. Love is the diamond essence of ourselves, ineradicable, unending, indissoluble. This innermost core, the heart of our being, is our deepest identity. It is a flowing presence that holds us and at the same time hurls us into the world. Love wants only to beam in, from, through us every day, everywhere, to everyone. Love wants to happen. All we have to do is not get in its way.

OUR SECURITY AND SENSE OF BELONGING ARE AT STAKE

How soft this prison is,
How sweet its sullen bars.
—Emily Dickinson

Little birds in the nest grow because they have the comfort of a parent's downy breast. But, when the timing is right, they also need to be challenged with a push out of the nest so they can fly as they were born to do. We too thrive only with that full combination of comfort and challenge. Yes, we can become addicted to what amounts to prison life as long as it offers comfort. The status quo becomes the very, and only, comfortable location for us. It presents no challenge: the other half of life we are avoiding.

Humans seek safety, security, and a sense of belonging—all appropriate goals. But the price is too high when it means restriction of our freedom to be ourselves or to undertake a necessary move. Most of us are not used to freedom, so we hardly notice how much of our personal life is designed to conform with what others require us to be. How tragic is a choice to be chained. Indeed, in this context there may be, unfortunately, both choice and chains. We forfeit one of the essential ingredients of humanness—freedom—in order to feel safe. That price is too high, unless we imagine the Declaration of Independence applying only to others, not to us.

This style of choice for chains applies in any area in which we stay too long in what doesn't work. As an employee we may not trust the possibility of abandoning a job even though it keeps draining our energy. In this instance we stay because we would feel unsafe and insecure without a continuation of what has become familiar. We associate familiarity with safety, and then safety trumps mobility. We may even stay when we are burned out, when we are depleted and nothing works to recharge us.

Safety and security describe trust. We needed to know that our parents would be there for us consistently and continually. When they were, we felt at home—and the comfort of home. We felt that we had been born into a trustworthy world. Such consistency and continuity of safety and security are goals we seek throughout life. The problem is that we come to believe that those two are allowed to dictate—and limit—our choices in relationships, jobs, memberships, and other circumstances. We believe they are the fair price we are required to pay. We then ask ourselves the wrong question: "Why complain?" We were not taught to check in with our bodies and minds to see if a situation was truly working. We were trained to be satisfied with what *seems real because it lasts*. That word *lasts* may translate in our life as "stay," another ill-fated association.

Why are safety and security so important to our survival? One reason is that our sense that we are safe and secure gives us access to higher brain centers. We make better choices when our prefrontal cortex can take executive charge. Without safety and security we are at the mercy of our limbic system with its sometimes faulty impulses and fear-based messages. When we trust our surroundings, relationships, and predicaments, we assess our world intelligently. Then we know the appropriate steps to take. When we are unsafe and insecure, our amygdala is alerted. The amygdala is a part of the limbic system in the brain that is a repository of memories of danger and abuse. It offers only primitive options: flight, fight, freeze.

On the other hand, at times freezing in place, staying put, may make sense. It can be adaptive for survival. An animal playing dead may thereby survive. A cave dweller may not become the prey of predators while remaining still and silent. Likewise, when abuse occurs, we might freeze our bodies and thoughts. Sometimes we distract ourselves into dissociation. We exit bodily consciousness and flee to a realm inured from the direct experience of pain. We imagine ourselves elsewhere but don't go there except by mentally dissociating from the unacceptable reality we are in. We learn we can survive *while* staying put in pain.

Freezing certainly happens in high-stress panic about a major change in our lifestyle, job, or relationship. But we don't have to go far, only out of what doesn't work on to our next step. It will take us into the unknown but not the kind of unknown that causes panic. It will be the unknown that produces wonder.

In high-stress situations we are also likely to misinterpret social cues. For instance, a neutral face might look angry. A beautiful face may look like it promises happiness. We are projecting from an amygdala-grasp base rather than from a cortical-accurate base. The amygdala operates on "grab what is appealing" or "shun what is unappealing," exactly the energies that Buddhism declares to be the causes of suffering. In the limbic world is "I want that" or even "I have to have that." This "must have" energy can mislead us. Within it is compulsion, a wily opponent of freedom. If we can shift our thought pattern to the prefrontal cortex, we can find: "It would be best to . . ." Now, there is a pause between impulse and behavior. That pause is our only chance at freedom. We can still act on impulses, but now we can distinguish between the ones that work in our favor and the ones that don't. It is that momentary "between" that makes all the difference.

In trauma, it is not only the bigness of the original event that impacts us. Trauma thrives on how much we are caught up in it. People at Ground Zero on 9/11 have a more severe trauma than those who heard about it a thousand miles away a week later. They may be sorry it happened but not carry trauma about it.

We can also notice that our limbic system sometimes presents false alarms when we are threatened or scared. Thus, though our hippocampus tells us a sensation hearkens from our past and is not truly dangerous now, it cannot convince the amygdala of that fact. In that part of the brain there is no past or future. Trauma is indeed anachronistic, treating the past as if it were present. The amygdala does not record timelines, which is why the danger seems so real here and now. We react to the past in the present and as who we were in the past rather than who we are in the present. The timing chain of readiness has not kicked in.

Mindfulness can help us. It is a prefrontal cortical experience. This is the part of the brain that can take time and think rationally. Its central executive network can be activated by a deliberate intention. We choose to let an incoming thought go rather than hold on to it. We do this over and over as we learn to be mindful, stay in the present without entertaining or restraining our thoughts and feelings. However, once we become adept in our meditation practice, that function of the cortex quiets down. We no longer need the intentional executive function quite so much. We begin to witness and let go of thoughts automatically. We have, in effect, wired into our brain a new way of handling thoughts and experiences. The same elements of our brain are in play but in new configurations. This is another progression in letting go of the hurtful past. Mindfulness is always a player in the theater of healing.

Mindfulness is paying attention to what real time is, present only. Then we are more likely to notice and access the fourth option that can follow fight, flee, freeze. It is *face*. We can face our fear demon rather than fight it off, run from it, or become a deer in its headlights. We can gradually stand and look directly into what has frightened us. That facing is also called *courage*, what was in us all along. The anachronistic power of trauma loses steam when there is nothing up for us but the present moment.

In that position of here and now facing there is no need for fighting, fleeing, or freezing. We keep in mind, of course, that some traumas are so overwhelming that facing is impossible, especially without a support like therapy. The sensory overload was too extreme and lasting. But we don't give up. We can practice approaching what is approachable in the trauma. Just that is success; we don't have to embrace it all, especially not all at once. We can permit it to appear or allow whatever in it we are ready to face. Facing without judgment or shame is what mindfulness can help us with. *When we stay with what is, it changes. When we stay with who we are, we change.*

The hammock of security can also be woven from concern for

financial dependency, our perception of age, or our experience of chronic illness: We are aware of the *financial* benefits or lifestyle goodies we are getting for staying put, and we don't want to lose them. A partner lacking financial independence may indeed feel chained to a relationship that does not work, seeing no alternative but to shelter in place. This person would easily move on if it were feasible. We can feel compassion for those who find themselves caught this way. Likewise, we may be in a job we don't enjoy; it has become a drudge. We find no challenge in it. There is no personal growth coming from it. But this job gives us a sense of security. We may be making enough money to pay the rent and ensure our lifestyle. We may also be in a work situation that has a retirement program, offers health insurance. Such perks can interfere with our readiness for change.

Age figures in too. We may have arrived at an age that makes a step out seem too scary to pull off. We may believe the dizzying stress of initiating a big change might be too much for us. Our advancing age may make giant steps close to impossible. We may remain in a marriage, remain under the same roof, remain in a religion or club while putting less energy into it. We are there and not there. That, in our minds, serves as the equivalent of an exit from what long ago ceased to work for us—and it is as far as we are willing, or perhaps able, to go.

Alternatively, we might have a chronic *illness*, and our partner, though now not appealing to us, is taking good care of us. This arrangement, in our minds, makes it worthwhile to stay put. We know the relationship isn't working, but at the same time, we appreciate the necessary help we are receiving in so reliable a way. Our partner seems glad to be of help and is not complaining. We don't feel we are taking advantage of our partner/caregiver, only continuing in a status quo that seems to work for both of us. We may nonetheless feel guilty that we are taking advantage of the time, devotion, and help a partner is giving us when actually we have ceased to sustain or fulfill each other emotionally. Yet, this is the only game in town for us. It is not as if we had a variety of options. Our opportunities have shrunk to a minimum. We stay because we believe there is no longer anywhere to go, and the only safe place is where we are.

WE ARE CAUGHT IN ADDICTION OR CODEPENDENCY

I shall come back to you who hurt me most.
—Dorothy Parker, "I Shall Come Back"

We might also stay stuck because we have become dependent or codependent. We are dependent when we rely on others more than we rely on ourselves. *Dependency* becomes addiction when we can't live without someone or something. Regarding alcohol or drugs, our dependency is on an ongoing irresistible craving. Our need then has become a compulsion. We want more and more as we are satisfied less and less. We build up a tolerance so we need more to find a high and then eventually never get enough to avoid a crash.

Addiction applies not only to substances but also to relationships, sex, romance, jobs, religion, affiliations with groups, or even attachment to a person. We have become tied to someone or something and can't let go. We feel we are getting a "fix" when we are with that special person or engaged in that special activity. We plan life around this person or situation. No matter how we try to go, we keep coming back for more. This is because there is no "more" that will ever be enough; we can never get enough of what we don't really need. Thus, we may stay in a relationship or situation that doesn't work for us or even hurts us. The characteristics of an addiction are evident in us: we have become obsessed with what we cling to, and we engage in compulsive behavior to keep clinging.

The more common experience of people who stay in what doesn't work is *codependency*. The word *codependent* originally referred to the partner's role in a relationship with an addict: "My spouse is dependent on alcohol; I am dependent on maintaining the status quo by covering up for her." Such enabling happens because we have become part of the addiction cycle. This helps us see why alcoholism is considered a family disease. Everyone is somehow in on it, often unconsciously. In this definition, the codependent is keeping the system of addiction in place. Codependency nowadays has taken on a wider range of meanings. It refers to a compulsion to stay in what doesn't work, to keep going back for more where there is only less.

This understanding of codependency refers to an excessive sense of loyalty, perseverance in what we have committed ourselves to but is no longer useful to us or others. Perseverance is a virtue, but it can mean running ourselves ragged for what will never pay off. Loyalty is indeed a virtue, but it can be used as a strategy to stay stuck. Loyalty leads to a sense of duty and obligation, central to the codependent mindset. Codependency combines and confuses duty and burden. We become so used to the combination we stay stuck: "I have to stay; it is obligatory. I can't go." In the healthy alternative, loyalty takes a "tough love" stance. It is based on acting in accord with the best interests of growth—ours or the other's.

In relationships and situations that have been or are abusive, we saw that we might have to exit them, but a subtle tie holds us back. That tie can be a form of codependency: We are hooked by our sense that we are *needed*, especially when our role in our family was to be the "helper." We might be proud to have that role, it's our way of being important, especially if it has always been our only chance to be important in the eyes of the others in our circle. Staying in a role, however unhealthy, gives us a sense of security. We fit in, belong. That may be why we stay so long in a role so thankless. It is understandable that we are unable to imagine any life-changing alternative. A loss of imagination is the price of being given a role and staying true to it.

Pity is sometimes an accelerant of codependency. We feel sorry for the other or others, so we stay in a relationship that has lost its verve and drive. We might feel sorry for our fellow workers if we were to give up our job. We might outgrow a group or project but believe we should stay because the others will be lost without us. These are examples of caring and compassion, but they are not adult versions of either. We are staying put as a way of showing our compassion to others but not equally to ourselves. Thus, it is not in keeping with an authentic loving-kindness practice, which always includes both ourselves and others.

Our challenge in all this—and in any issue regarding leaving a situation that doesn't work—is to find a way to *transition supportively*. This means we go in a way that maintains our connection to those we leave behind: "I go on loving you but can't live with you." Such a declaration is a full *yes* to our own reality but with full caring for others too.

An often overlooked element of pity is remaining aware of our side of it. We know we will feel bad when the other person feels bad. That could be a central motivation for pity. We might stay in a bond because to break this bond will mean not only that the other person will suffer because we are going but that we will suffer even more watching the other do so. In this instance we know the other has tugged at our heartstrings, and our bond has taken on a sentimental tie that keeps us stuck. The healthy alternative is a relationship in which we are each committed to helping the other face reality squarely. We are not with one another to make it all nice but to keep it all real. Then pity does not figure in, while compassion does. Pity stops us both; compassion galvanizes us both.

Here is a chart that may help us see the difference between pity and compassion:

PITY	COMPASSION
I may look down on you because of your predicament.	I see you as an equal since we all take a turn being in unfortunate situations, a given of life.
I may judge you for your woebegone state.	I am not judging only assessing what your needs are.

PITY	COMPASSION
I am categorizing you.	I show respect for your uniqueness.
I feel I can be in control.	I support your self-empowerment.
I am over here and you are over there.	I am in here with you.
I am feeling sorry for you as a victim and try to fix things for you. I want everything to come out right for you.	I am feeling sorrow for your circumstance and join you as you work through it. I am not responsible for making it all come out right for you in the end.
I mostly see your predicament.	I see you the person.
I am concerned about you, and it leads me to caretake you.	I am concerned about you, and I will support you in caretaking yourself.
I will do all I can so you don't have to experience the full brunt of your own pain.	I am offering a space for you to have your experience safely and securely.
I feel guilty if I don't make you my priority.	I care about you but maintain my boundaries and take care of myself too.
This is my emotional state.	This is both my authentic feeling and my spiritual practice.
I stand in for you as a protector.	I stand by you as an ally.
I focus on or become overly engaged with your personal distress.	I am looking at ways to confront the conditions in society that lead to pain and inequity.

PITY	COMPASSION
I am not happy until you are. You so occupy my mind that I can't get back to my own life easily.	I feel with you but go on to what is next for me without being driven or stopped by feeling bad for you.
I am tied to you.	I relate to you.

The first five entries on the left side of the chart describe the main negative qualities of codependency.

We may be tied to the belief that we "have to see things through to the end." I recall in adolescence that once I started reading a book I felt I had to make it through to the end even though I had lost interest in it. This is a simple example of how something inside us keeps us engaged in what no longer works. I had become codependent toward authors of uninteresting books! (I don't recommend reading this book to the end unless you are getting something out of it.)

If we redesign our sense of loyalty in a more balanced way, we might describe it this way: "I stay with what works until it does not. Then if it seems worth it, I do all I can so it will work. When that does not work, I let go and move on with love and without judgment."

Our loyalty may be a way of appeasing those who have abused us. The Stockholm syndrome refers to the tendency of some victims of kidnapping or other crimes to develop positive feelings toward their captors or abusers. For instance, at times when the captor is bringing the kidnap victim food, the criminal will be viewed as kindly rather than obliged, so positive feelings may increase. In addition, a victim will have negative feelings toward the rescuing authorities, such as the police or social services. The victim is so allied to the persecutor that the rescuer becomes the bad guy! The sequence of abuse, submission to it, and appeasement to induce mercy has been observed in other primates. This may substantiate that bonding to stay safe indeed has a survival dimension.

Ultimately, the syndrome tells us about trust. The victim comes to trust the persecutor and distrust the rescuer. There is no final research regarding the Stockholm syndrome, but the fact remains that any of us might love those who hurt us. It is an ironic turn on the Sermon on the Mount: "Love your enemies." Here it is not a sign of a spiritual commitment but the result of a psychological victimization. Along these lines, by the way, I recall that Martin Luther King Jr. said that he was glad that Jesus did not say "Like your enemies." That would have been a tall order. We can love more easily than like. Loving is wanting the best for others—for example, health, joy, enlightenment. Liking entails being drawn to someone who pleases or attracts us. We don't have much control over that.

Stockholm syndrome, like all trauma, usually hangs on even when the victim has returned to a normal routine. This is the post-traumatic stress syndrome or what I call the *ongoing* traumatic stress syndrome. It had a beginning but not yet an end. We stayed too long in confusion and delusion. Now it will take time to see clearly again. This applies to any experience of overstaying in what hurts us. It will take time to restore ourselves to clarity and composure—like the earth after an earthquake.

We can also understand the drama in a codependent relationship by looking at our fascination with *suspense*, the essence of entertainment. We keep watching a movie because it has garnered our curiosity about how things will turn out. Each scene is constructed in such a way as to make us wonder what will happen next. The word *suspense* is from the Latin for "hang." We are hanging on, uncertain, breathlessly awaiting an outcome, hoping it will be the one we wish for. Suspense is the twin of expectancy. The anticipation of "more to come" is certainly built into the human psyche. It applies to our own story, chapter upon chapter. Our need to see how things will go makes us less likely to go. Suspense itself can become our focus, even addictively so.

The partner in a relationship that is suspenseful becomes our drug of choice. We remain in suspense about our ever-unfolding drama.

What will he do next? When will she do something different? What will happen now? What will change? Just as we stay put in a theater because we are in the grasp of suspense, we stay put in our lives. Such addiction to drama fuels codependency and keeps us stuck in what doesn't work. The concealed irony is that *standing still is moving away.* We think we are staying put because we want closeness when all the while we are distancing more and more.

Codependency often happens in a family. We can keep in mind, however, that it is not codependency to have a legitimate concern about how our family or children will react to a move we may make. It is a sign of caring when we take their reactions into account as we make our plan. We don't want to create so enormous a kerfuffle that others will suffer. We want to respect the timing of others as well as our own. We know it is not fair to those we care about to spring something shocking on them. Their readiness has to be honored, just as ours must be. We have to take time to work toward our self-revelation so others can receive it safely. We will still do what we need to do but without trespassing on others' sensitivities. This is not procrastination, but rather only respect.

In a codependent relationship, we have gradually come to believe that we can't go at all until our partner is OK with it. Likewise, we can't make a move until our family approves. This way of operating is not respect; it is a way of staying stuck. We might, in this context, also wonder if our motivation is truly other-centered. It might be that we are using our "concern" about everyone else's reaction to hold ourselves up.

Here are some summary characteristics of codependency:

- We wait for change rather than make a change.
- We don't have a bottom line for how much we will put up with. We let others trespass on our personal boundaries, both physical and emotional.
- We want everything from those who can't—or won't—give us anything.

- We believe we owe others even when they give nothing or very little or too little in return, not even thanks.
- We act out of obligation not choice.
- We have become so dependent on a partner, association, or job that we believe we will fall apart without him, her, them, or it.
- We keep going back to the dry well, each time with a bigger bucket.
- We keep hoping for more and more when we are only getting less and less.
- We are feeling hurt or disappointed but keep sitting still for it. (Codependency is so puzzling; it can seem as if we have a *need* to be victimized.)
- We can't ask for amends from the one who fails us since we don't believe that person should ever have to face consequences.
- We excuse our stuckness in abuse by using the word *love*: "I know he hurts me but he loves me," or, "But I love him!" Yet, for adults, love is real only when it works in healthy ways for all concerned.
- We mistake love for an attachment that has become familiar—and so feels good. Then the strength and endurance of our clinging fool us into believing we really do love the other. It is that kind of "love" that keeps us stuck—what real love would never do.
- We find ourselves at the mercy of our fear of loss and abandonment. We then feel compelled to keep coming through in codependent, overly committed ways for the other. But if we look more carefully, we see the real motivation, our fear of being alone, our fear of loneliness, a lack of trust in our own independence.
- "Nothing better will ever come along!" This is probably the saddest reason to stay stuck codependently in something that has ceased to work. We doubt we will be able to attract a new partner, find another job, a new affiliation, a better situation.

We imagine that what is going on right now, no matter how unsatisfactory, is all we are capable of finding or worthy of having.

- An experience of abandonment in early life can mislead us into believing we are obliged to put up with anything in order to keep the other with us.

- When we are imploring someone not to go, we are saying that otherwise we will be nobody.

- When we had to move from house to house often in childhood, we may now mistakenly equate staying put with stability.

- We fail to believe the old adage "Rejection is direction." In other words, once we are turned away, we are—wonderfully—looking in the direction of what can come next for us. Is the fear of just such a new vista behind our tangled thoughts and paralyzed limbs?

- We hang on to a relationship because we don't see the difference between someone who really wants to *be with us* and someone who only doesn't want to *be without us*. The message we are getting is: "I won't hold you, but neither will I let you go."

- We are committed to keep doing all we can, rather than all that is appropriate, for others. No matter how much we give or do, we rebuke ourselves for not doing enough. We feel shame and inadequacy even when we are doing more than what is adequate or required.

- Regarding our children especially, we might also be intent on making sure that everything comes out as we think it should for them. We can't let them have their own story with all the "heartache and the thousand natural shocks that flesh is heir to." We think we should intervene and give them a smooth ride through life.

- When others do not like us and act unkindly toward us, we believe we must have done something wrong. We feel shame rather than indignation. We then do more for them rather than just say "Ouch!"

- Avoiding guilt is a primary concern: "I'm unhappy but at least I am not guilty."
- We can't let go of guilt about a past transgression though we have made reasonable amends. We know that no one can change the past, but we believe we are required to pay for it for the rest of our lives.
- The one we coddle will wind up *expecting* our self-sacrificing behavior rather than appreciating it. When we are rebuked for not doing enough even though we have done all we can do, the ricochet of self-blame is complete.
- When someone is in need, we can't easily say: "I can't help you with this, but I can direct you to those who can." We just keep infantilizing the other by caretaking to an extreme.
- We believe we are permanently indebted, so we feel we are being greedy or selfish if we ask for what we need.
- We can't be happy unless the other is happy, and it is our fault if the other isn't.

Yes, there is a path to freedom from codependency. An option many people have found useful is joining a twelve-step group such as Al-Anon or Codependents Anonymous. Therapy, self-reflection, and journaling also make a difference. Usually, it takes a spiritual program to heal us because we need refuge in a power beyond our own ego—the secret founder of codependency. For too long, we have relied on our own efforts rather than realizing that our partner or coworker is beyond our control, that is, beyond our ego.

- A program helps us learn to let go with love.
- We find a new definition of love, not in an all-giving me but as a mutual giving and receiving.

- We confront the fact that we have been overly responsible, another way to stay stuck. We find reasonable ways to act responsibly in our relationships without being compulsive about it or imprisoned by it. We keep our commitments but not at the cost of our own boundaries or our need to move on.
- We are liberated from guilt about never having given enough.
- We state our boundaries and ask that they be honored.
- We ask that the other join us in a healing change—not wait for us to make a change.
- We never give up on others but accept the given of life that some people resist repair. That does not make us push harder. We grieve it and stay at the ready if they arrive at a turnaround.
- A combination of therapy and a twelve-step program is a state-of-the-art avenue to release us from codependency.

I add an encouraging synchronicity: Last night I watched a documentary about Guatemalan bishop Juan José Gerardi, assassinated in 1998 for his humanitarian work. Afterward, I felt inadequate as a person because I am living here in comfortable Santa Barbara doing my writing and teaching rather than engaging in heroic actions. In the midst of my self-reproach I also reminded myself that I am certainly making a contribution to others, but my inner critic pooh-poohed the value of my work in comparison to that of heroes, martyrs, and saints.

I woke up this morning pondering all this. When I opened the internet, lo, I came upon an article about the "vow of stability." In monastic traditions, Christian, Hindu, and Buddhist, some practitioners take a vow of "stability of place." This is a commitment to stay in the monastic community for the rest of one's life. Here staying put is a spiritual practice! This vow is based on trust that *where we are is exactly where we can achieve enlightenment and sanctity*. This same morning, I also found this quotation from Dutch psychologist Han F. de Wit: "This is my place, my situation, and that is what I want to work with, however it develops. . . ." I was immediately struck by how the author was addressing my previous night's concern directly and in so timely a way. Indeed, I felt the quotation to be a personal message to me to appreciate my work and life situation as they are. Gratitude for the graces I receive—and share—is an antidote to lamenting their inadequacy.

We are always facing the question of whether something is working, that is, effectively doing what it is meant to do. Sometimes we see that we are staying in what doesn't work at all or not enough. And sometimes, as in my story, we see that something is working after all. Then we can let ourselves off the hook and feel content. In the next chapter I attempt to show how this can happen. And it can happen, no matter what our predicament or how forcefully we have been trained not to let go as soon as possible and to endure as long as possible.

TWO

What Helps Us Move On

So long so stuck
In toils of taut taboo,
Now may I wave
Like wind-inspired bamboo.

IN CHAPTER 1 we explored how and why we might become stuck. In this chapter we look at ways to become unstuck, how we proceed on our journey through life.

Sometimes we are triggered into moving on by people or situations. Things get so bad, our limitations no longer figure in. We walk into any unknown, all fear gone. However, the opposite can also be true. The situations or relationships do not become bad enough to force a move. They are stubbornly mediocre, insipid, dully dragging on—and us with them. *Things will never be so good as to make us want to stay; they will never be so bad as to make us have to go.* Such relationships and affiliations remain poised on a fulcrum of ambivalence. But as we've seen and experienced, living in ambivalence for prolonged periods can be painful and stifling—and we don't have to stay there forever. We can engage in practices and build resources that help us dive off the bored board. They are the topics of this chapter.

If there is a fear of falling, the only safety consists in deliberately jumping.

—Carl Jung

FINDING SECURITY WITHIN OURSELVES

How stand upright
In this quaking world?

When we lack safety and security, we fear that we won't be able to handle what may happen in our lives. Out of fear, we may try to take control of whatever comes our way. In contrast, a yes to our present reality as it is and work on dealing with it can become the fulcrum for stability. We can leverage access to our inner resources, our powers to handle any way the chips are landing in our lives. "Handling" means that we will not be defeated by fear but have our chance to do all we can about our predicament and grow from the experience. Our goal is to let the chips fall where they may and make the best of that.

We no longer have to fear that all will fall apart if we don't maintain tight and widespread control. We see that the opposite of control is simply a resolute yes to reality, to what is. In that yes is liberation from the grip of fear and its twin, the need to be in control. We no longer require the sense of control, which was a paper tiger after all. Armed only with yes, we ask no exemption from the given of occasional powerlessness and not having all come out as we want it to.

Likewise, most of us treat feelings and beliefs about powerlessness as absolutes—accurate descriptions of ourselves or of what is happening. Fear is a feeling that does not necessarily portray a truth. Powerlessness is a belief not necessarily based on a reality. When we don't make these distinctions, we are cornered, imagining ourselves as having no options, no resources. Then, by years of habit, we imagine that gaining control of others and of life situations is our best option.

Let's distinguish *power* from *control*. Power is the right and ability to make choices that have an effect and may influence others. Control is power over others by restraining or forcing them. We control others to maintain our sense of personal power. But this isn't power at all, only domination. A commitment to equality is what can move us to a true empowerment. That will mean no more need to control. How ironic it is that we believe control of life or people to be the sword of power that will offset our powerlessness. Actually, it is the last-ditch—and futile—effort of the powerless. It is bullying others as fear has bullied us. The real weapon against incapacitating victimization is no longer listening to "fake news" about ourselves. The fake news is not that we are or can be powerless; it is that control cancels our powerlessness and puts us back on top. Two self-evident facts of life are that everyone feels powerless sometimes and everyone is powerless sometimes. In other words, no one is on top all the time. Gaining control is not the solution. The real remedy is saying yes to the givens we all have to live with and then picking ourselves up, dusting ourselves off, and getting back in the game. This is self-restoration, restabilizing ourselves, the truly useful remedies. We don't need to fear being powerless—instead it can become the portal supreme into activating our powers.

Our fear of powerlessness, of not being in control, is ultimately a fear of vulnerability, a fear of grief, and a form of self-doubt. Handling each of these three is how we gain a healthy sense of personal power. Let's look at each in turn:

REGARDING VULNERABILITY: Insisting on being in control may mean trying to make ourselves impervious: "You can't hurt *me*!" We associate helplessness with giving away our power, with submission to those in power. But it can be just what it is: the given that sometimes we are helpless—and so what?

REGARDING GRIEF: We know if we don't get our way we will feel sad. To avoid that grief we insist on having everything come out as we want it to. We can practice grieving what we lose, eventually seeing it as a skillful means of resolving our grief rather than storing it in our bodies.

REGARDING SELF-DOUBT: We fear having personal autonomy—the ability and right to live in accord with our own deepest needs, values, and wishes. We are afraid we will not have, or do not have, what it takes to handle what may happen if we are not in a relationship or affiliation that defines us. We are terrified of being open to surprises or moving into territory uncharted. We might also suffer from "imposter syndrome," believing we are frauds though we have clear evidence of our initiative and skills. To build self-confidence is to wade through the quagmire of stuckness. Then self-doubt vanishes.

Albert Camus, in *The Stranger*, writes to all of us in an encouraging way: "In the midst of winter, I found there was, within me, an invincible summer. And that makes me happy. For it says that no matter how hard the world pushes against me, within me there's something stronger— something better pushing right back." The pushback does not take courage; it evinces courage. When fear attempts to bully us, we retort: "But wait! I trust I am always stronger than my scared mind reports." This courageous confidence grants us access to resources of safety and security in ourselves, rather than only in relationships with others.

We began the process of separation and individuation, our two poles of development, in childhood when we took over, one by one, the functions of our caretakers: We crawled across the room rather than be carried across. We tied our own shoes rather than have our parents tie them. We fed ourselves, clothed ourselves, held ourselves. This gradual assumption of tasks readies us to move from dependency to autonomy and then to interdependence.

A health-promoting family provides us with a base—that is, a launching pad. Yet it also provides us with a refuge; we can go home again if we need the embrace of those who will welcome us gladly at each of the chapters of life. We recall our analogy of the little birds launched into the spacious sky but only because they were cared for

and comforted first. The self-defeating alternative is not to launch ourselves but to stay in our parents' home when we are adults capable of
moving on to live our own lives. Our parents are then not launching
but nesting us. They are enabling our stunted development, though the
ultimate responsibility is still ours. Yet, no matter what our success at
completing developmental tasks, we humans can't let go of our need
for safety and security. From that stubborn fact comes the dangerous
option of buying them with our own pain. This happens when we lose
confidence in our own inner resources. We can't locate safety and security within; we become needy for it from others. Then we are disabled
from taking action when suffering becomes our lot.

We notice that the reasons we stay in situations that don't work
are always somehow based on faulty equations to which our minds
have consented. We equate two realities that don't have to go together.
For instance, as we have discussed earlier, we may equate enduring
pain with success in getting through life, hurt with love, the presence
of others with safety and security, staying put with loyalty. It doesn't
have to be this way. We can scuttle equations that don't foster our
evolution. We have already practiced this: as health-conscious adults
we have broken the connection between nicotine and necessity, between junk food and fun, between physical beauty and candidacy for
intimacy.

In healthy early child-rearing, our parents were not trying to mold
us into what they thought we were supposed to be. They were, instead,
excited to see who we came in as. But in other experiences of childhood, perhaps we had to earn acceptance at the price of our own true
self-presentation—another faulty equation. Now in adult life we might
be adapting ourselves to the needs or expectations of others. Often
what was not safe to do or be in early life feels unsafe in later life: We
overvalue acceptance from others. We imagine it is necessary if we are
ever to be loved. We crave acceptance and try to earn it, sometimes
waiting too long for it to happen. We might sexualize acceptance or try
to garner it by giving up our own autonomy.

We don't blame ourselves for any of this. A deficiency from childhood naturally turns into an insatiability. What was missing before we can't get enough of now. A need has become neediness: "What I crave shows me what I always needed but never did find satisfactorily." We know which of our needs were not fulfilled in early life by noticing which ones we now want too much or can't get enough of even when we do get too much. Our neediness actually tells our story. We keep wanting more, never believing we have enough. Likewise, we then make choices that are not in the best interest of wholeness. But wait, there is a solution: we can grieve not being accepted in the past and look for the means to find it now in healthy ways, especially in ourselves. We cultivate this when we can begin to understand the given of life that some people accept us and some don't. We come to believe that we can survive, even thrive, in either instance. We can say yes to the loss of what was missing by grieving it rather than by finding a scarecrow substitute for it.

An excessive thirst tricks us into being sure we see an oasis, though it is only a mirage. A fervent interior longing can likewise trick us. Our longing seduces us to grab on to something exterior that we are sure will satisfy us. We believe that what we need is out there instead of in here. We all make this error, and it is nothing to be ashamed of. Likewise, a longing can be tricky because our capacity for fulfillment may be smaller than what it will take to fill it. *Can I accommodate a cornucopia?*

Our practice is simple: We mindfully notice each time we are sure that satisfaction is only to be found in *that* over *there*. Then we turn the mirror to ourselves and say, "I will first trust *this here*, what is in me." If later we want to supplement the "this here" with a relationship, we will choose that candidate very carefully. It will be the one who mirrors us back to our own inner resources, appreciates them, and wants to join us in building them. Such people will not be the ones who congratulate us for being lucky enough to have found them. They will instead be the ones who are so in tune with us that there never was a need to find them. It all just happened—like creation.

We have made reference to *needs* and *neediness* in this section. Here is a chart that may be helpful in distinguishing them. This chart shows two extremes. We can also be somewhere in between. Moreover, there are times in our lives when we may be needy, no matter how psychologically healthy we are. We should also keep in mind that we may not be needy even though we may come across that way. This will be something to check out with those we interact with on a daily basis.

The Difference between Need and Neediness

Healthy need can be defined as a requirement for a project or relationship to thrive. Neediness is the state of requiring fulfillment and reassurance to an extreme degree.

A PERSON WITH A HEALTHY NEED . . .	A NEEDY PERSON . . .
Comes across to the other as open and welcoming.	Comes at the other with a must-have energy.
Can be satisfied with fulfillments that happen sometimes.	Has to be satisfied all the time, can't get enough.
Appreciates the other's response to a bid for fulfillment and can take no for an answer.	Is frightened or rejected by a lack of response.
Can trust when the other is trustworthy.	Can't trust fully.
Is not trying to get from someone now what was missed in childhood.	Is trying to get from someone now what was missed in childhood.
Has inner resources to fall back on no matter how things turn out.	Lacks inner resources so has to find them in the other person; lacks self-reliance or the ability to reconstitute after an ending.

A PERSON WITH A HEALTHY NEED . . .	A NEEDY PERSON . . .
Self-nurtures, self-stabilizes, self-regulates.	Can't self-nurture, self-stabilize, self-regulate.
Has independence and seeks interdependence.	Is dependent to the extreme.
Seeks relationship for enrichment.	Seek relationship for survival.
Does not require constant assurance.	Requires constant reassurance.
Is totally OK when alone.	Can't stand being alone for long.
Respects the other's need for alone time or distance.	Cannot handle the other being alone or away.
Is able to miss the other without having to make contact.	Is unable to tolerate absence.
Is OK with periods when the other is absent.	Takes any absence as abandonment.
Will stay in touch but not too often or in an invasive, interruptive way.	Has to have constant contact—e.g., texting or calling throughout the day or perhaps stalking.
Does not have to know the other's whereabouts at all times.	Has to know whereabouts at all times.
Holds.	Clings.
Asks for a hug and seeks affection sometimes.	Demands being held often and has to be given constant affection.

A PERSON WITH A HEALTHY NEED . . .	A NEEDY PERSON . . .
Enjoys sex when it is mutually desired.	Has to have sex more than seems reasonable.
Honors limits and boundaries.	Disregards limits and boundaries.
Is OK with a moderate amount of attention.	Requires full focus rather than sharing the stage.
Will be assertive about expressing needs: asks.	Will be aggressive about getting needs met: demands.
Is glad the other has a circle of friends.	Sees the other's friends as rivals and may suspect they are trying to take the other away.
Can handle the other having special closeness with special friends.	Will react with paranoid jealousy.
Is not easily triggered.	Is continually triggered.
Stands.	Leans.
Is ready for an intimate relationship.	Will have personal work to do before being in a relationship.

I will come to you, my friend, when I no longer need you. Then you will find a palace, not an almshouse.

—Henry David Thoreau

CONFRONTING OUR SELF-DECEPTIONS

We might deceive ourselves into thinking all is well when nothing is. We might trick ourselves into thinking there is hope when we see no evidence of it. We might guess a relationship will improve when all we have to go on is wishful thinking. We all think like that sometimes; it comes with being human.

As we have been seeing, we can't allow ourselves to know what isn't safe to know. We can't act when it isn't safe to act. This is not cowardice; it is good sense. Our psyche protects our vulnerability by seeking safety and security first of all. Only then can it let us confront, process, and resolve an issue.

Though we sometimes can't allow ourselves to know what is really happening, we might at least feel hurt, anger, or frustration as sensations in our bodies. It helps to admit the ongoing inner "ouch!" to ourselves and to someone we trust to give us helpful feedback. We can then more easily see if we are deceiving ourselves into thinking our relationship at home, at work, or in any affiliation is really working.

With respect to deceiving ourselves about the health of a relationship, we can know whether it is working by using a checklist of the five *A*'s, the components of healthy need-fulfilling love: attention, affection, appreciation, acceptance, allowing. These are meant to be exchanged between one partner and the other. We can ask ourselves if this is happening:

ATTENTION: Each of us is showing attentiveness, an engaged focus on one another's feelings, needs, and concerns. We really hear one another. We read between the lines when one or both of us are distressed about something.

AFFECTION: We are showing affection in accord with the nature of our relationship. In an intimate relationship this includes sex and/or other forms of physical affection. Among coworkers or clients at our job it includes kindness and emotional support without the component of physical intimacy.

APPRECIATION: We show mutual gratitude rather than taking one another for granted. We value one another, cherishing each other's individuality. We are firmly together but acknowledge our independence too.

ACCEPTANCE: We accept one another as we are, limits and all. To accept is to welcome our partners just as they are. We take someone into our heart with both dark and light characteristics. We are nonjudgmental. In this sense, accepting is being mindful—a spiritual practice.

ALLOWING: We are not restricting one another in the pursuit of each one's own version of happiness. This is allowing in the sense of supporting autonomy. We do not need permission to be free. We have the Bill of Rights for that. Allowing as a form of love is acknowledging and saluting our freedom. It is the opposite of controlling and interfering. Allowing also refers to our emotions. We trust that the whole spectrum of human feeling is welcome and can be expressed in our own unique ways.

We have a sense of safety and security when we feel loved—when we are receiving the five A's. This happens in a holding environment, that is, one in which we have a secure attachment. This is just what the five A's foster. If we do fall apart at times in our relationships, we restabilize through receiving the five A's from those staying with us as we go through it: "I am looking for the pieces of myself that I have mislaid or waylaid. Your love is helping me find them."

The five A's are a signature, unique to each person; there is no standard, no one size fits all, and each A has to be individualized in accord with how a partner can and wants to receive it. Matt shows affection to Betty exactly the way he has shown it to all the other women in his life. But Betty wants affection that is personalized, her own brand of touching and holding. This applies to all five A's in any intimate relationship. Both Matt and Betty also want attention, appreciation, acceptance, and allowing *as each needs and understands it*—not off-the-rack, but tailored. It is, of course, up to each of them to let the other know what that will look like. Then it will take a capacity and a willingness to love someone in a unique way—the only way love can happen. We can see how crucial readiness is in all this. (In seeking a partner, we want someone who is already or close to or working on being ready for what it takes for intimacy and commitment to happen.)

Intimacy happens when we give and receive the five A's at the same time with the same person/people:

- *I know you love me when you give me these five* A's—*attention, affection, appreciation, acceptance, allowing.*
- *You know I love you when I give them to you.*
- *When we receive them, we feel loved.*
- *When we give them, we are showing love.*

In childhood we need the five A's all the time. In adulthood we need them *only in good enough ways and only most of the time*. Needing in those two ways is how we know we are being adult in our relationships. This is also the key to letting go of unreasonable expectations for "more," "always," and "perfect."

Are we in a relationship that works? Each of us can ask ourselves the following questions. When the answer is a resounding yes, we have a relationship that works. When the answer is a resounding no to all the questions, the relationship is not working:

- *Am I with someone who truly pays* attention *to my needs and feelings?*
- *Am I accepted as I am?*
- *Am I appreciated for what I do and who I am?*
- *Am I receiving the* affection *I long for?*
- *Do I feel allowed and encouraged to live in accord with my own deepest needs, wishes, and values?*

We may fool ourselves when we can't reply to the questions at all. Instead, we keep saying: "I don't know if this is working." If we have been saying that for a long time, it isn't working. Self-deception is then interfering with our knowledge and powers. We are, in other words, not giving ourselves the *A* of allowing ourselves to know our own truth. We might be unable to see that the time has come to let go of something that ended long ago. It is difficult for any of us to take the advice we hear in *King Lear*:

> The weight of this sad time we must obey,
> Speak what we feel, not what we ought to say.

GENTLING THE INNER CRITIC

> As you left their voice behind
> The stars began to burn
> Through....
> —Mary Oliver, "The Journey"

Our *inner critic* is the part of us that has given up on us. It hurls "can'ts" and "shoulds" at us: *You can't go. You can't make it alone. You should stay put.* The inner critic is a mindset, usually from the past; it's something we learned, not something we were born with. It is an echo from people and institutions who judged us in the course of life. They include family, peers, religion, school, society. This mindset is now internalized and part of our mental apparatus. Most of us have internalized some shaming messages from our past. The inner critic most often has the voice of the scolding parent. This voice takes on a life of its own in us, so we think we are hearing our own accurate assessment of ourselves. But we are actually listening to a skilled ventriloquist. Yet, there is good news. Since the critic now exists only in our heads, we can change the message we hear. We can input the voice of a nurturing parent or kindly coach instead, one who says what encourages us and bolsters our self-esteem. We can hear in our mind what we wanted to hear from our original parent. We might also hear what our parent or any supportive person in our lives has said. Nurturance can be described as a caring that is shown by the five *A*'s—sources of joy too!

We can tame or silence the inner critic—this enemy within who tells us we can't move, can't make an accurate assessment or a wise choice, that we have no options. We do this not with a whip but with gentle coaxing of the negative voice onto the channel of self-advocacy. Free of self-deception we might say to ourselves: "So much of what I hear from myself is not really me. I allow my supportive voice to have a say."

One inroad into the posture of the inner critic is noticing that the voice always sounds final: *this is who you are and all you are.* It is absolute in its verdict: *you are nothing but guilty or weak or inadequate.* It is not provisional. It is not open to discussion, to solutions, to alternatives—exactly the style that can keep us stuck. Indeed, an inner critic abhors the idea of a journey; it wants only to keep us immobile, unevolving. In other words it is nothing less than the bully of fear. This is why it can't be right in what it whispers to us. The inner critic is on the side of self-reproach, self-abnegation, self-negation, self-loathing. It does not love us. Likewise, the inner critic moves from one particular experience to a deadly generalization. "She doesn't like me" becomes "I am unlikable." Thus, what happened today becomes tomorrow's decree. The inner critic is the heretic who denies the Buddhist teaching on enlightened liberation being available to everyone all the time.

Six Practices to Change the Inner Critic into an Inner Ally

Here are some ways to reset our inner critical voice into one of self-advocacy. Choose any one or try one each day:

Moving from Past to Present

List three negative messages from your inner critic in your journal. Connect each statement to its origin, usually in early life. Was it appropriate then? Is it appropriate now? What shame did you feel? Where did you first hear this? Who said it? Were they trying to help or hurt you? Do this without blame for anyone but only as an accessing of information.

Moving from Always to Sometimes

Notice if the inner critic's vocabulary is absolute: *You always . . . You can't ever . . .* Under the absolute statement write a more inclusive one. Don't deny the main point but only reduce it from absolute to relative: "Yes, I often can't . . ." and "Sometimes I can . . ." Now you are changing a negative verdict against you into a neutral fact about all of us. You are reminding your inner critic—that is, yourself—that inadequacy is a feature of being human. It is a given that all of us *sometimes* make mistakes, act inappropriately, fail. Let yourself thereby feel a kinship with all other humans. Remind yourself that you also are committing yourself to do what you can to make up for your failings—all that really matters. As Joe Biden said at the 2020 Democratic Convention: "Failure at some point in life is inevitable but giving up is unforgivable."

Mindfully Breathing

Place the message of the inner critic into a mindfulness container: Sit with the statement and shear it of judgment, shame, belief, insult, triggering. Let it become only words in your head and label them as such. Do all this as you keep coming back to your breaths, lifelong teachers of taking in and letting go.

Showing Self-Compassion

The inner critic disregards the pain it causes us by its put-downs. It does not seem to care about how our feelings are hurt, how our self-esteem is diminished. We can, however, step in and show self-compassion as the antidote to its judgments. We are actually helping our inner critic become compassionate. Our practice also extends to the inner critic in us that judges others, whether internally or vocally. In that area too, we convert judgment into compassion. Everything we judge others for has some kind of pain behind it. Our practice is to look for the pain the other might be feeling in doing what we believe is wrong. For instance, we judge someone as controlling. Behind that behavior there can be the pain of compulsion and fear. We are retraining our brain so that our inner judgments automatically redirect into compassionate avowals.

Giving Equal Time

The inner critic catastrophizes about upcoming events and sees the worst as what will definitely happen. We then worry about the outcome. Worry can be reduced by openness to other possibilities beyond the catastrophic. As a practice, we expand our speculation: We give equal time to the opposite of catastrophe. We acknowledge that the worst might not happen. We hold our hands out palms up and imagine we are holding the negative speculation in one hand and the positive in the other. We look at the hand holding the positive and see ourselves being grateful. We look at the negative one and see ourselves being courageous in handling whatever happens. Now we are allowing our minds to go in two directions, but in both we find something positive.

Calling on Our Spiritual Resources

Call on the spiritual resource that fits for you. Ask for support in your practice:

> *Bodhisattvas, help me appreciate your wisdom and compassion.*
> *Holy Spirit, I thank you for your gifts, help me appreciate them and put them to use.*
> *May the universe join me in my personal evolution.*

Here are three examples of combining the above practice with these spiritual resources:

Inner critic: *You make stupid mistakes because you are stupid.*

Your sane voice: *Like all humans, I sometimes make mistakes. I also make up for them when I can.*

Your higher self: *I have received the gift of wisdom. May it keep opening in and through me. It is opening right now in this practice I am doing and being.*

Inner critic: *You will never amount to anything.*

Your sane voice: *Like all humans, I will sometimes be successful and sometimes not. I commit myself to do all I can to live a worthwhile life.*

Your higher self: *I am of great value to myself, others, and the world. May I deeply grasp this and be thankful for it.*

Inner critic: *You have nothing to offer a partner or a career.*

Your sane voice: *Like all humans, I have some valuable qualities. I will keep gaining knowledge and skills. I have no control over whether someone will see them, but I will keep showing them.*

Your higher self: *I have all the effulgent virtues and graces that any human may have. I also keep upgrading my skill set to fulfill my calling. May I be thankful and keep sharing my gifts with the world around me.*

We don't have to worry too much about buying into our self-deceptions. Our higher self is unrelenting in its battle against pretense. Circumstances and people will keep appearing on our stage that will unmask the characters and plot. This will feel threatening to the imperious ego robed so safely in its thousand disguises. But a subtheme of this book is letting go of an inflated ego, the harbinger of a great fall, so let's welcome the opportunity.

This book offers many practices and proposes many changes in how we relate to ourselves, others, and our world. None of us will be perfect or totally successful in establishing new mindsets and behaviors without work on ourselves. In addition, a readiness has to happen that is beyond the reach of work. One of my greatest joys is knowing that I am more and more of a beginner and being friendly toward that position.

> My pilgrim's progress has been to climb down a thousand ladders until I could finally reach out a hand of friendship to the little clod of earth that I am.
> —Carl Jung, response to a student who had just read Bunyan's book and asked Jung what his "pilgrim's progress" consisted of

HANDLING REGRETS

> Familiar as an old mistake
> And futile as regret.
> —Edward Arlington Robinson, "Bewick Finzer"

Regret is the inner critic's favorite sport. Regret is lamenting about past choices that we now consider to have been mistakes. Since the past can't be wiped out, neither can regrets about it. Our work is not to get rid of regrets but to handle them mindfully and usefully.

We can begin by realizing what happened in the past does not have to be taken as the whole picture. Regrets serve to keep us stuck because the inner critic mutters: *You have made so many mistakes because you are inadequate and unskilled. You are too messed up to work anything out or try something new.* This is, of course, the voice of fear, the king of all regrets. Once we accept the given that we all make mistakes, fail to act, impulsively and unwisely choose, then regret is no longer about shame. It is about saying yes to our human predicament with all its intriguing intrigues. As we just discussed, we are looking at givens of human experience and thinking they refer only to us. Indeed, regret thrives on isolation: *Only I could have been that dumb.* Actually we have *all* been that dumb and worse. Our compassionate sense of ourselves in this frail human family makes regret less impactful. In that context, regret can help us cultivate the virtue of humility.

In addition, regret is about grieving. The root word *gret* means "grief." We keep spinning our wheels in our grief experience, never resolving it. That is why regret keeps gnawing at us. We repeat rather than complete. All our errors and losses can find their way to grief, then to nostalgia, then to letting go. When we interrupt this protocol, we wind up stuck in regret.

Using our journal, we can work with regrets by seeing how they may relate to our life themes:

We take all our regrets, annoyances, bad luck experiences, mistakes, and ask how they fit into the tapestry of our whole life, how we made something useful from them. This will reveal a coherent theme in our life, a personal myth, a uniqueness we came in with but may not have dared allow ourselves to know.

We pay special attention to finding the features of ourselves that we repressed, disavowed, or refused to acknowledge. This may feel dangerous. We ensure our safety by practicing in total privacy. We murmur: *I will admit my dark side now just to myself.* This releases a liveliness we may have been keeping imprisoned without knowing we were doing it. Here is an example: We honestly question how and if we have loved authentically in the course of our life. We will admit that some of what has passed for love of others was really controlling or possessing. We may follow it up with a conversation with the people involved in which we admit the agenda we had over the years. Today we want to upgrade our way of loving so that it is sincere. The confession will also help cultivate humility, the most appealing of all the virtues.

We can practice *futurizing* a regret: We shift from putting ourselves down for our errors to appreciating the growth that has resulted from them. We then promise ourselves a future in which we will be careful about not making the same mistakes. We design a future that will be wiser. *We have moved from being victims of the past to being students of it.*

WORKING THROUGH OUR HELD-OVER GRIEF

After you've gone there's no denyin'...
You'll feel blue....
—"After You've Gone" by Henry Creamer, Turner Layton,
    Ray Sherman

These lyrics convey a meaning we rarely pay attention to. They remind us that grief follows *all* departures, no matter how bad or how good the situation was. We are built to mourn any ending. Even graduation from high school meant the end of friendships that had blossomed but were now about to fade or vanish. We were excited by what might be coming next and so not in touch with our natural grief about that ending. When I think back now to my own graduation, I recall the girls crying at the ceremony, something we boys dared not do. Yet, now I realize the girls were the healthy ones. They were going with their grief, giving it voice and tears. That is the way to go through anything, positive or negative—*with* grief. It is not the kind of grief that stops us, only one that smooths a transition and gives a sense of closure. It is grief as processing a change. All transitions require attention both to an ending, grief, and a beginning, excitement.

At the end of painful chapters of life, we are, of course, glad to be released. Yet there is still grief. We are not grieving the end of the untenable predicament we have finally put a stop to. We are not sorry we finally left what couldn't work. Our grief is a holdover from the start of the chapter when we were so convinced that this connection would surely be perfect for us. We are grieving the crashing of our *original hope* that the relationship, career, affiliation, or belief system would really work as it seemed to promise. We are grieving the disenchantment of our expectations that a good experience was awaiting us. We are also mourning the crash of our idealized version of what a partner or affiliation would offer—e.g., happiness. We are mourning a fact that very soon became too obvious to push aside: we were in something that was not going to work no matter what. We may not have called it grief—we may have dubbed it disappointment or some other emotion—but it was grief nonetheless. Our body was surely in stress mode, thus acknowledging a grief denied in our minds.

No one wants to feel grief about an ending we foresee so close to the beginning of a relationship or career. We are likely to talk ourselves out of it. But the grief does not vanish. Like a mole, it goes underground that is, into our unconscious. It waits for its time to surface. The final ending is that time.

When we first feel a sense of emptiness in a relationship or affiliation, we might presume it will fill in on its own. That makes sense on a new moon night but doesn't work for our human phases. Mourning awaits: sadness about a loss or disappointment, anger that what we were led to expect never happened, fear that there is no way out now that the die is cast: "I am married now and I can't just jump ship this soon." "I just started this job and can't quit this fast." "People will laugh at me if I go now since they will see what a mistake I made by getting into this."

Finally, after years of dislike, we find the career or job that really fits for us. We soon—overnight?—forget the former one. Years later, we retire from the new career we have so enjoyed. Yet, upon retirement, we feel sad. Some of the grief is for the ending of the job. Yet we notice there is more sadness in us than can be accounted for by the retirement. We may finally be feeling the grief from the earlier realization that our first career was hopeless. Silent grief has saved itself up and spoken up on its appropriate occasion.

How can this happen? We might be engaging one or more of these three negative options:

Losing Hope

We had hoped for a sterling experience, but now our hopes have dropped like lead. It's well-nigh impossible to feel grief fully at the beginning of something. Our natural tendency is to tell ourselves: *It will all work out. It will get better.* We deny our hopelessness in favor of a hopefulness that is only wishful thinking.

Feeling Powerless

We believe we can do nothing to change our situation. We may keep trying to revive what died at birth. We are fueled by wishes. When nothing changes for the better, we may become angry and turn on a partner or colleagues. We may fall into despair, becoming depressed and listless. We no longer care what happens in this prison of silent screams.

Becoming Lost in Distractions

We might comfort ourselves with new healthy choices while remaining tied to one that does not work. We may turn to addictions or other forms of escape that are unhealthy. In a relationship, we might have an affair during this phase. In a job, we might slack off or cut corners. We might take advantage of career perks in an unethical way. In a religious affiliation we might become bitter, believing we have been duped.

A highly valuable practice is to look back over each of the chapters in life and take for granted that every one of them had grief at its ending. We can ask ourselves if we felt it or ran from it. If we ran, our unshed tears are still waiting in line for their turn to flow. We can let ourselves feel our sadness now—it's never too late. Some of our grief may have been released over the years without our noticing. Many of our new tears are ones from the past, now adding volume to those of the present. Crying during a movie may not only be for the character who touched us but also for all the times in life we needed to be touched and weren't.

I share a story here that combines our topic with the mystery of timing. We will see how timing is related to synchronicity, meaningful coincidence. At age twenty-seven I was visiting my friend George who took a phone call. While waiting, I looked at his copy of *The Little*

Prince. I opened it at random, and my eye zeroed in on a sentence he had underlined: "It's such a secret place the land of tears." I remember being struck by the sensitivity of that statement. I could tell it had profound meaning, but I also understood that it contained more depth than I was capable of comprehending at that time. I knew I was still too young to have toured the land of tears enough to explore its enigmatic geography. Nonetheless, the sentence stuck in my mind ever after. I guess now that I was saving it for a time when I would be mature enough to grasp its import. Over these fifty years many tears have come and gone I have gradually plumbed its basic meaning, as perhaps the musings in these paragraphs exhibit.

Every ending has tears. The only question is when they will be released. Our natural response is to weep aloud; our habitual escape might instead be to sweep our grief under the rug. When we allow our tears, we complete our grief and move on to what is next for us. *Is our fear of going on the real reason we avoid our grief?*

Some griefs shout to us, for instance, the untimely death of someone close to us. But there is also a silent grief that churns deeply within us without our even guessing it is there. Grief is related to love; we grieve the eventual loss of what we love or loved. This line from the poem "Ephemera" by William Butler Yeats says it well: "Our souls are love and a continual farewell." Yes, since it is a given of life that all is impermanent, grief is a necessary skill. There is always something passing away or passed away, so there is a farewell in all our hearts, always at the ready.

When we don't attend to a grief at all, we might find ourselves years later still in its grip. It is suddenly triggered when a similar event occurs. Then we wonder why we feel so bad about losing something not so terrible to lose. We might even feel a disproportionate reaction when we give up something we are not at all sorry to see go. We don't name it; we can't, as that would open too overwhelming a Pandora's box. We are being tugged by past grief that was never given a hearing, let alone allowed to name itself. Griefs wait their turn—and always take it.

Give sorrow words. The grief that does not speak
Whispers [to] the o'erfraught heart and bids it break.
—Shakespeare, *Macbeth*

THE SORTING PRACTICE

We can no longer afford to equate faith with the acceptance of
myths about our nation, our society, or our technology.
—Thomas Merton, *Faith and Violence*

An often overlooked way our past affects our adult life and choices is
our imbibing of attitudes, biases, and beliefs that we hold on to without
question throughout our lives. Many were smuggled into our brains
by family, school, religion, and society before we had the capacity to
critique or even notice them. We took on and held on to what now we
might want to upgrade or toss. Some of the inherited attitudes have become driving forces, governing principles of our life and our behavior.
They are debris from the burned-out homestead of the past now piled
up under the foundation of our present home.

We sometimes hold on to other-designed definitions rather than
ceding them to the past. These are cultural myths, outmoded views,
social conditionings. They have become so much a part of our sense of
our own identity we hardly notice them, or in fact, don't notice them
at all. We might even consciously hold on to them imagining they are
necessary to maintaining a coherent sense of self. For instance, we were
taught that the world is orderly. We have often heard ourselves saying:
"There has to be an explanation." This presumes there is always a reason
for what people do or what happens. Likewise, finding the explanation
to what perplexes us endorses our belief that we are in control—again.
Such a misreading of reality presumes people are always rational in
their decisions and actions. That is something we can now question
with a big smile, given our lifetime of experience.

Loyalty to our childhood religion gives us an example of something to question now: I might believe that still being somehow, somewhere, somewhat the Catholic I was taught to be is necessary if I am to continue being David. How much of holding on to that identity subtly keeps me tied to the biases and restraints it carries in its wake? Going on, in this instance, means upgrading faith so it is free of the myths Thomas Merton warns us of.

In Plato's *Apology* Socrates says: "The unexamined life is not worth living." An important adult task is to examine the imports we received in order to find out which ones still fit for us. We can examine the subtle and obvious contents of our minds and keep what reflects who we are as upright adults, while chucking what is no longer, or never was, appropriate to us as people of intelligence and integrity. This sorting practice will take careful inquiry and discerning examination. It may require dialogue with confidants or a therapist. Journaling also helps.

Sorting can't be done all at once; it will take years to explore the myriad souvenirs in our psyches. This is because the messages are mostly not explicit. They are now in the realm of unnoticed programming and conditioning from sources we might now oppose.

There are two kinds of sorting: *absolute* and *relative to circumstances*. Regarding the absolute ones, our choice is total-keep or total-toss. Regarding the relative ones, we decide to keep or toss depending on how they stack up to what is useful for an adult life today. Let's take an example in the total category: When I was in middle school, my mother took me to buy my first suit. As we looked at the choices of colors and styles, she told me: "David, always choose a suit you can wear at a funeral." That advice goes to total-toss, no prejudice against Mom.

Here is an example that shows how the choice may not be absolute but relative. In kindergarten our teacher had us line up in the corridor. She gave three orders: 1. "Form a line." 2. "Keep your place in line rather than trying to get ahead of anyone." 3. "No talking in line." We can ask ourselves now which of the three rules we choose to hold on to. We can easily sort them: 1 and 2 we keep; 3 we half toss. We realize that the advice of 1 and 2 represents useful and necessary behaviors for a lifetime in a culture that respects lining up. We also realize that "no talking" was about our not disturbing the students in the other classrooms. Thus, it does apply throughout life but only when talking might disturb other people. At the supermarket, the DMV, or the train station we choose to stay in line but certainly know we are free to chat with the person ahead of us or behind us. In a setting where others are working nearby and need to concentrate, we either don't talk at all or talk very quietly. Thus, we have a half-toss for rule 3.

In the following list are some check-in areas that help us with the practice of careful sleuthing/sorting to see which messages we still want to follow and which to let go of. The messages are stated below explicitly, but we need to remind ourselves that these messages and others like them were mostly implicit and unspoken when they came through to us. We will ask which of these are useful in some way, so we may choose not to toss them totally.

Family Messages (Including Ancestors)

Remain attached to your family no matter how they treat you.

You have a specific role in the family and you can't veer from it, e.g., the role of caretaker.

You are more than or less than your other brothers or sisters, or than anyone.

If you step out of line, your parents, the authority, can punish you any way they want to. Parents have the right to abuse you.

You have to be like your parents or choose the future they want for you.

You have to keep working whether you want to or need to.

You can't embarrass the family by getting divorced.

Hold on to biases regarding those you were taught to disparage or look down on.

Be and show your full self at your own risk.

You can't question parental authority.

How much of my own truth was scared out of me?

School Messages

Stay loyal to school values and biases.

Don't stand out by being different

Only your final grades matter, not growth into becoming a
free-acting being or embracing values beyond academics.

Becoming a good student and citizen means obedience.

You are here to memorize not think.

Don't ask a lot of questions.

Follow all the rules at all times.

Be and show your full self at your own risk.

You can't question school authority.

What of myself was schooled out of me?

Religious Messages

Stay loyal to the religion of your childhood.

The religion you are in is the only true one.

A patriarchy is and has to be in charge.*

Women do not have ownership of their bodies.

God is male.

Happiness is a reward from God because you have been good, and
suffering is a punishment by God because you have been bad.

It is wrong to have sex before marriage or to engage in self-
pleasuring at any time.

If you notice gay impulses, don't act on them ever.

---

* Many women remain loyal to a religion that denies them their rights, prohibits
them from having authority, and shows itself to be misogynist in manifold ways. Why
would women stay put in an atmosphere like that? One possible, and unfortunate,
answer is that they have become accustomed to being used and abused by men at
home and elsewhere, everywhere. When we are only safe in a life of obedience, we
don't believe we deserve freedom or respect. We surrender to the rules at the price of
our own interior liberty.

Be and show your full self at your own risk.

You can't question ecclesiastical authority.

What region of my imagination was shut down?

Societal Messages

"Allegiance to the flag" means "My country right or wrong."

"With liberty and justice for all" does not apply to all of us.

White people are superior to all others.

War is justified, and it is a duty to sign up for it.

Patriotism means obedience to what the government dictates.

Don't take a stand against the established order or policies.

The planet is here for our use and so are the animals.

Getting ahead, no matter what it takes, is legitimate and
    praiseworthy.

Money is our central goal, worth, and purpose.

A good and happy life is the result of material possessions.

Hold on to biases regarding those you were taught to disparage
    or look down on, especially when voting.

Be and show your full self at your own risk.

You can't question governmental authority: "To obey is life; to
    disobey is death." (Yes, President Calvin Coolidge really said
    that. I saw and heard him on film, and I replayed it to be sure
    I heard correctly. Also, I noticed he spoke with arrogance and
    incontrovertibility, as if he were giving us all fair warning!
    To be fair, though, he was referring to a specific crime, not
    declaring an overall philosophy—at least not explicitly.)

What was drilled into me or out of me before I knew how to
    sort?

We can decide consciously which messages help us toward wholeness and which ones do not. Some we can outgrow without effort.
Some will require our addressing, processing, and resolving. Some may
not make an exit no matter how menacing the bouncer.

Writing our list of messages in a journal may help us see at a glance which ones we want to keep and which we want to let go of. We can place these lists on side-by-side pages in our journal. We can rewrite the list of the ones we are letting go of on paper and then burn them. The "keeps" are nothing less than affirmations of who we really are.

We know we have become our authentic selves when we keep what we want and let go of what we don't want. We live our lives accordingly. The no-longer-useful has been properly disposed of and what is of value we thankfully cherish.

Some of us *internalized* others' version of who we were supposed to be. We took on their description of us and have remained true to it. This is a form of staying put that is subtler—and more poignant—than any encountered in this book so far. *Our most deep-rooted, our most unnoticed addiction is attachment to our false self, the one we have been until now: "I need to, have to, be this guy I think I am."*

The self before sorting out true and false, the self conditioned so surreptitiously by so many well-meaning or not so well-meaning sources, that is the one we may still most desperately cling to. It is crafted and carefully preserved because it alone seems to hold the passport to safety and security in a world that fears—or kills—diversity.

From a Buddhist perspective, there is no self at all—not visible, not deep within. But this self of mine is not an opponent of that no-self. This is the actor-I, the one I play in accord with a script not my own, the one designed to make sure I will be liked. This is not the face I had before I was born. This is the imposter-face I donned as soon as I noticed it was dangerous to be who I was really born to be.

It is hard to locate fully—lodged in apps, extensions, and preferences hidden from my view. But the spelunking sorting practice—provided it is fearless, ruthless, and thorough—is the skillful means to find its hiding places. Then what will make a personal appearance will be a real me, not this wooden boy I was carved to be. I will discover what Shakespeare called my "unknown sovereignty."

Can I be brave enough, live long enough, to turn *me* loose?

I end this section with a personal story that shows how sorting can also refer to choices about location. A friendly man with an orchard leaves his extra fruit out for us neighbors to take. One day the owner was present as I took two plumcots (cross between a plum and an apricot) from his basket at the side of the road. They were unripe and quite hard, so I asked: "Do they ripen off the tree?" As I walked home I heard myself repeating my question, guessing it was an important metaphor about me. So I changed it to: "Would *I* have ripened off my family tree?" My answer was unhesitating: "Absolutely! I could not have matured, lived in accord with my unique needs and longings, found my true calling, if I had stayed put on the Richo compound in my native Connecticut. I ripened three thousand miles away in California." That move away, leaving home, is necessary for some of us, yet staying near home can work for other people quite satisfactorily. My metaphor is, of course, strictly personal and not state-related. People can certainly ripen in Connecticut, just not I. Later that day I chuckled to recall the motto of Connecticut, now so appropriate to me: "He who transplanted, sustains."

A WEEK OF MEDITATIONS ON GOING

Here are seven quotations on our topic of taking leave of what is ready for a change. A useful practice is to ponder each one slowly and meditatively day by day for a week. Let the quotation speak to you personally, exploring how it fits into your present life circumstances. In your journal you can write your responses to the questions that follow each one.

Sunday

There came a time when remaining tight within the bud became more painful than the risk it took to bloom.
—Diary of Anaïs Nin

How and in what areas of my life right now do I feel restrictions
from outside myself?

How and in what areas of my life right now do I feel constrictions
from inside myself?

How are restriction and constriction familiar from my past,
including in childhood?

What region of myself am I afraid to set free?

What form of suffering do I fear awaits me if I show myself as I
really am?

If I were to bloom into my full self, what would I look like,
personality and lifestyle-wise?

Who would welcome my flowering, and who would fear it?
How can I appreciate one and assure, or move away from,
the other?

What am I waiting for? Let me name the ducks that have to line up.

He is [you are] wooing you from the jaws of distress to a spacious
place free from restriction.
—Job 36:16

Monday

Leaving home is half the Dharma.
—Milarepa

How is my childhood still affecting my adult choices?

Did I learn how to tolerate pain from my father or mother, and
am I doing this now?

What happened in my early life that now holds me back from
taking action?

How can I take full responsibility for my present predicament?

Who were the people in my life who helped me evolve, and how
can I validate their confidence in me now?

What attitudes did I buy into that now immobilize my get-up-
and-go energies?

How can I now respond to the evolutionary drive in me, the one
that has always been in me, to let go and go on?

How can I appreciate and respond to the many saints and
bodhisattvas cheering me on right now?

Tuesday

To go with the drift of things,
To yield with a grace to reason,
And bow and accept the end
Of a love or a season?
—Robert Frost, *Reluctance*

What is drifting off in my life now?

What do I feel as I see it go?

Is it scary to face it?

What might I be overlooking?

How can I surrender gracefully to what needs to change in my
relationship, job, affiliation?

If I were to grieve what has already ended, how would it move me,
how open me?

How can I hold all I love and need to leave in a heart-space?

What keeps me here?

What beckons me to go, to stay?

What would it look like to bow to the Buddha—that is, to the
light hidden in my present circumstances, a light ready to
shine on and through me?

Now I understand why there is a world and me. It is so that a
hidden light can reach into me from seen things, then through
me to all I see.

Wednesday

We know that we will have to burn to the ground in one way or another and then sit right in the ashes of who we once thought we were and go on from there.

—Clarissa Pinkola Estés, *Women Who Run with the Wolves*

What in my life now is ready for the fire that burns away what is no longer working?

What in my life now is ready for the fire that enlivens?

How willing can I become to letting something or someone go?

What did I think of myself before and how has that image or belief changed?

What did I think of my relationship before and how has that changed?

What would it look like if I were to "sit right in the ashes" of who I have been?

How do I "go on from there"?

What are the inner resources waiting to pop open when I renew myself?

What frightens or empowers me about going?

Thursday

New experience has become more secure than security.

—Daniel Lindley, *On Life's Journey Always Becoming*

What do safety and security look like for me?

When in my life did I feel truly safe and secure?

Do I feel safe and secure today?

Would a whole new experience scare me off?

What would it take for a new way of living to become appealing to me?

What am I willing to try that would make my life at least a little different or better?

Are there resources in and around me I can turn to?

Who are the allies of my transformation?

Friday

It is more worthy to leap in ourselves,
Than tarry till they push us.
—Shakespeare, *Julius Caesar*

How might I be waiting for something to happen that will force me to move?

Does someone in my life have to make the first move before anything can change? How did that person get into such a role?

What will it take to open my inborn capacity for taking the initiative?

How can I feel compassion for myself when I hold back and at the same time ask for the grace to take a step forward?

What is making me wait for permission to leave what doesn't work?

How will I feel ashamed or guilty about making a move? How can I put those inhibitions aside?

Is there a way to make a choice now rather than waiting for the courage to do so?

May I trust that my whole courage-body is geared to make a journey.

Saturday

Fear is the mind killer. Fear is the little death that brings total obliteration. I will face my fear. I will permit it to pass over me and through me. And when it has gone past me I will turn to see fear's path. Where the fear has gone there will be nothing. Only I will remain.

—Frank Herbert, *Dune*

What fears are holding me back from what comes next on my journey?

How can I face my fear and still stand upright?

How can I let my fear pass through me like lightning through a lightning rod?

May I let my fear go to ground, trusting Mother Earth to take it and release me to walk freely.

How can I let fear go and let freedom in, or rather, out?

What will it take for me to believe I will survive making a move, even thrive thereafter?

Who are the allies, both mortal and immortal, I can trust to accompany me as I walk through the dark valley?

Can I believe I never walk alone?

THREE

When We Feel
We Just Can't Stay

The meaning of this great journey would remain quite
mysterious, but with a glimmer of hope that somewhere
in the distant future "we" might figure it all out.
—Rabbi Arthur Green, *Radical Judaism*

SOMETIMES WE GIVE UP when there is still a chance for a remodel, a
change, an improvement, a resolution. We walk out the door before
the gift arrives. This gift is reinventing a relationship, a job, a situation, or even ourselves. We might abandon ship before we find the
advantages and benefits we never guessed were stowed away there.
We sometimes feel—often bodily—that we just can't stay a minute
longer. That can indeed be true; we have reached our limit. But at
other times our need to leave can be mistaken for a frustration that
can indeed be resolved. We are failing to see opportunity—only unsatisfactoriness. In this chapter we look at what is behind our need
to go or run, our feverish desire to get as far away as possible from
a person, work situation, religious or group affiliation, indeed any
circumstance we find ourselves in for what seems to us too long. In
the next chapter we will explore ways to work on things, to find the
tools that make a difference.

CONFUSIONS IN CLOSENESS, COMMITMENT, AND AUTONOMY

A relationship to individuals or in affiliations and jobs is real when it is a *close committed connection that simultaneously ensures individual autonomy*. Let's look at closeness, commitment, and autonomy and how they can be integrated so relationships, associations, and situations can work.

Adults have learned to interweave closeness and distance in their relationships at home and work. This combination accommodates the needs that arise in our bonds and respects our individual needs too. There is no problem in our wanting distance, only in how we try to attain it. The healthy way will be to ask for it directly: "I need some space right now. This is not about you but about my own need, and it will be temporary." The alternative, unhealthy style is to create a conflict, fight, or uproar that automatically ensures distance. Most of us have a thousand ways to get distance when only direct address is really needed.

We sometimes look for ways to sabotage closeness because we realize it will entail our becoming vulnerable. We might think: *If I let someone get close, all my inadequacies will stand out. The persona, self-portrayal, I have carefully constructed so that people will see only my good side will crumble. My embarrassing shadow side will come into view.* Letting all we are come into view is indeed vulnerability, but it is also an entry into true closeness. When we hide, we are forfeiting our chances at being lovable and loving, the pinnacles of a human life. Being vulnerable in a relationship does not mean letting ourselves be victimized. Intimacy involves *voluntary* emotional vulnerability, an opening of the heart so the other can see us as we are. A healthy relationship combines closeness with concern for personal boundaries. This can happen when we match the extent of our vulnerability to how trustworthy the other person is.

Vulnerability means opening interiorly, so it requires an atmosphere of safety and security. With voluntary and boundary-protecting vulnerability our inner resources grow, and we can handle hurt feelings or betrayal rather than be destabilized by them. Paradoxically, this kind of vulnerability strengthens us. When our fear of closeness disappears, we appear. Is our fear of closeness, after all, really a fear of making a full-on personal appearance, stage fright and all?

Fear of close connection can also be a sign that we don't trust someone, though we may not notice that consciously. We feel on an intuitive level that the other person will take advantage of our vulnerability, use it against us. Then our fear has a positive purpose. It helps us guard our sensitive self from those who might betray, shame, or take advantage of us. An inner wisdom tells us who and what to trust ourselves to. Some people can be trusted to love us; some can't be trusted because they won't love us but only hurt us. Then vulnerability becomes victimization.

In a fear of commitment we might imagine intimacy as invasive. We don't want to forfeit our chance to take our leave when we believe we need to. A real commitment is an engaged fidelity to someone or something we trust. It means working things out when conflicts arise. It includes mending, restoring, reestablishing a broken connection. It is a promise to maintain a connection even when that project becomes quite trying. Then, paradoxically, our bond, no matter how frayed, can bolster our resolve to stay the course. If our needs are consistently not being met in a relationship, it does indeed make sense to go, but *if our needs are met in a good enough way most of the time, staying through thick and thin makes sense.*

A commitment also involves staying in a relationship with a person or circumstance when our needs are temporarily not being met. We don't run when a partner is in the hospital and not there to attend to our daily requirements. The word *temporarily* is, of course, key. We may tolerate what is temporary; we need to question what has become permanent.

Commitment also includes a series of kept agreements. That too may seem to debit from our personal liberty. We may feel we are living in obligation rather than choice. There is a way of working on that: We make only the agreements that we know we can keep. Sometimes that will mean agreeing to do what we may not want to do. A commitment requires just such fidelity to the needs of the bond rather than only to our own. Then we automatically act from choice. When we feel a sense of heavy obligation, we are not really in it by choice. That sense of being forced to stay rather than enthusiastically choosing to stay will, hopefully, make us uneasy. Then we ask ourselves what we really, freely want and go from there.

Our fears of closeness and commitment are reasons we may not stay long enough in a relationship or circumstance that can work—and the opposite of this might also be true. We may be hesitant to present ourselves to the world as independent adults. This is fear of personal autonomy, stepping into full mature adulthood *while* relating to others.

Autonomy means living in accord with our own deepest needs, values, and wishes. We are self-directing and self-governing. We have a sense of agency in our world. We have a sense of personal authority over our beliefs and choices. We can bravely express our own ideas, opinions, and perspectives. We are comfortable in our own skin. We are at ease in having standing in society or anywhere as independent persons. We have a healthy self-trust. We are comfortable with power. We know it is important to use it wisely. We have no guilt or shame about having it.

In relationships at home or work, in memberships or affiliations, there are, of course, always boundaries. Adults with autonomy respect limits. We maintain our own sense of human sovereignty within legitimate and reasonable parameters. We are sovereign but not supremacist. We respect the autonomy of others while maintaining our own, even if that takes defending it. We understand that interdependence is the appropriate goal in all relationships and connections, but that does not interrupt our personal liberty. A good analogy is in the relationship between individual states and the federal government of the United States. Each state respects federal guidelines but insists it also has specific rights that can't be overturned by the national government.

In intimate relationships we may not realize that we have a fear of independence or that it can be as strong as the fear of closeness. If our childhood was about obedience, it may be difficult to believe that we can make our own choices in adulthood without having to look over our shoulder all the time. When we are unsure of ourselves as truly free beings, we might resort to unskillful ways to establish our autonomy. We wind up with a bogus version of it, one that means license rather than freedom. It is then an adolescent style, not an adult one. For instance, we become overly competitive, push boundaries, act out, break agreements. These look like instances of distancing, and they are. But at a deeper level they may be clues to self-doubt and insecurity about having or showing our independence. Such fear of losing our autonomy is ultimately doubt that we really have it.

Here is another subtle connection: We will never really know our needs in a relationship until we are free enough to know ourselves. Needs are requirements for personal growth, but only an individuated person can grow. We will fail to achieve intimacy without autonomy. We have to be someone before we can be a partner to someone else. That is the paradox of all connections and the key to success in any bond.

We have connected fear of closeness or fear of commitment with fear of losing our liberty. What if this were merely a foil for the real fear in us: fear of our own autonomy? Closeness and commitment can't really take away our freedom. What if our real fear is of the adult challenge to balance closeness and freedom? Now we find ourselves in deep waters but, fear not, we can still swim.

Let's also notice the social dimension in the dance of freedom and togetherness. Our problem as primates is that we feel closest to those we are most like: our family, team, colleagues, fellow sports fans, fellow religionists, political allies. Such limited and limiting loyalty can lead to division, prejudice against those who are different from us, the xenophobia that opens the door to aggression. Indeed, our cuddly hormone, oxytocin, works in two directions: It makes us close to those we love, but it also can make us averse to people we don't know. We like those whom we believe to be like us, but we distrust those whom we see as not like us. What helps us out of such ingrained prejudice is getting to know and spend time with those who are different from us. The loving-kindness practice in the next chapter can also help. Once others are not so other, we can get close without fear and mistrust. We then move from "only us" to all of us—a spiritual victory indeed.

Nature designed us all differently—even at the fingerprint level. Since all that nature does is for an evolutionary purpose, it must follow that we can only survive and thrive in diversity not uniformity. Likewise, and on an even more hopeful note, consider this analogy: Mother Nature gave each of us a musical voice type, for example, tenor, bass, baritone, soprano, alto—the required constituents of a choir. So nature must have wanted more for us than self-satisfaction; she wanted harmony too.

Finally, we remind ourselves that fear is the master of trickery. It has us coming and going. We fear closeness *and* we fear autonomy. Fear makes us stay too long in what doesn't work and likewise not stay long enough in what can work. When we free ourselves from the grip of fear, we stun the bully who won't allow us to go and who stops us from staying. We can open a door and cross a threshold alone and then stay in a *living* room side by side.

THE PETER PAN FLIGHT PATTERN

Puer aeternus is Latin for "the eternal boy." It is a term found in the ancient Roman poet Ovid's *Metamorphoses* and refers to the god Iacchus. He is associated with Cupid, Hermes, or Pan—all forms of the trickster character in stories. The trickster archetype refers to the energy of fooling others by giving one impression of an identity but actually being its opposite. For instance, Cupid may coax us into love at first sight but then take away our honey in one fell swoop. In more modern times we see him in Peter Pan.

Carl Jung referred to the eternal boy as a negative feature of the child archetype. An archetype is a common theme or way of being that appears universally in human experience. The *puer* is the archetype of the charming, fun-loving, devil-may-care man who, psychologically, has never grown beyond adolescence. These are qualities that can be enormously entertaining to a partner or prospective partner. Someone may stay because of the liveliness a partner displays so abundantly. Since the *puer* also has obvious maturational deficits, someone may also stay to fix him. Both these reasons to remain with what ultimately is not working can apply in any relationship or connection. We stay for the liveliness; we stay for the chance to rescue.

The ever-boy lacks the adult capacity to be responsible, hardworking, goal-oriented, or able to make a lasting commitment. He can't stay anywhere for long—that is, long enough for a workable relationship to flourish. This is why the *puer* archetype fits our discussion.

But this archetype is not limited to men. When such qualities appear in females, we shift to the Latin word for "girl"—*puella*. She can be found in myth as Kore, the maiden goddess. But the same archetype can appear in nonbinary people with a combination of traits. The pattern has been well-defined in Dan Kiley's book *The Peter Pan Syndrome: Men Who Have Never Grown Up*. His other book, *The Wendy Dilemma*, treats the female aspect of the archetype.

The eternal boy lives with an optimism that someday his ship will come in without his having to work the sails. There is always something *about* to happen, something just around the corner, that will make all his dreams come true. There is never a *plan* to make something happen or engagement in the ongoing work that might bring it into being. There is always a pot of gold at the end of the rainbow, but he never has any coins to show for it.

The *puer* thinks of dedication to a person or task as a form of confinement with no chance of escape. For instance, the eternal boy insists on moving around rather than settling down—to him a form of restriction. Responsibilities are then constraints rather than pathways to responsible living. The reason hard work is not appealing to him is because another unconscious drive warns the *puer* that success is dangerous. It might lead to having obligations, rather than license to do as he pleases in the adolescent version of adult freedom.

The ever-boy evinces our compassion when we realize he does not operate out of choice. He is at the mercy of unconscious drives that direct him to cut corners, find others who will smooth his path, manipulate to get his way, do what feels instinctively pleasing rather than what is responsible, seek only his own gratification. At the same time the *puer* does not know his true feelings. He therefore vacillates from one fantasy or behavior to another and wants to take others with him on a wild-goose chase. The *puer* will disappear in a relationship, but he will come back. He will fly with his lady on his back, then leave her stranded to wing off away alone, only to return with a new story about it all. This style explains why the *puer* is called a Peter Pan. Author J. M. Barrie associated him with the nature god Pan, the half goat known for playing panpipes. In fact, the original staging of *Peter Pan* had him appear on stage with pipes and a live goat.

We can see why aficionados of the *puer* stay stuck. Anyone can be seduced by the Peter Pan style—so charming, so assuring, so adrenaline-rich. His partners find themselves mired in a relationship of promises that don't pan out. His style is to seduce and then withhold. But his lovers have convinced themselves it is worth the wait. A partner might also fail to see a *puer*'s manipulation: he induces us to follow suggestions contrary to our own best interests. That is how we finally lose.

In relationships, the *puer* wants the perfect partner, but since there is no such thing as perfect, this functions as a shield from ever committing to real live human intimacy. The *puer* might be satisfied only with a woman as eye candy. She will at the same time be required to take care of *his* needs with no promise that he will return the favor. He may be wealthy and not need employment. He may be needy but does not earn a living wage since he believes he is special, destined to soar above the workaday world. The *puer* trains a partner or friend to become a caretaking parent, bankroller, or servant of his needs—and he finds new ones all the time.

One of the ever-boy's main characteristics is taking chances. He keeps defying the rules and imagining there will be no consequences. This may look like courage, but it actually reflects his sense of entitlement. He believes he leads a charmed life and will be safe no matter what dangers he may risk. Others may die of cancer from smoking, but that can't happen to him because he has immunity from what medical authorities warn about. In fact, for him there are no authorities.

What no one easily notices about the carefree man-boy is that he hides a deep wound inside. His dashing flights are meant to make up for an inner void he never allows himself to acknowledge. The movement toward health for the *puer* would entail a terrifying descent into that abyss as deeply as he ascends into the sky of getaway. He would benefit from seeing into the dark corners of himself, but this will take a comeuppance, the archetypal work of Hermes, the main trickster god in Greek mythology. Usually, however, the *puer* is only the Jack who will be nimble as he jumps over the light rather than into it.

The eternal boy-god in ancient times was also a symbol of the transition from death to life. The god Hermes was honored as the guide to the underworld, the journey through the dark into the dark. The *puer* can awaken from his slumber in entitlement and find new life through a direct encounter with this gloom of pain and grief—just what he has so successfully evaded all his life.

The fear of facing one's own suffering is a fear of not having inner resources, a distrust of oneself. The *puer* suspects this deficiency in himself but acts as if it were irrelevant. How others see him is more important than growing up—that is, building and trusting his inner resources and taking his chances at maturing. This is the work that can move him from flying to staying. Only then is authentic bonding possible.

IT NEVER WORKED TO BEGIN WITH
AND IT'S NOT WORKING NOW

In some instances, both in relationships or in the workaday world, the need to work things out does not apply. It will be a waste of time and effort to keep working on a relationship or to stay in a job or affiliation if we never have felt fully comfortable in it. We were always uneasy—and are so now. This was not because we feared commitment but rather the situation never seemed suitable for making one. There were always problems that proved insurmountable. There were continuing concerns that could never be fully laid to rest. We always had doubts about whether we were cut out for this particular relationship or association we were in. This led to less and less engagement. We were not ready or able to put our whole heart and soul into our job or association with a group. We felt less and less connected.

Here are examples of how any of this might happen in an intimate relationship:

- More and more, we partners find ourselves engaging in activities separately. Sometimes we even exclude one another.
- We were never really compatible in our interests and still aren't.
- There is hardly anything now we enjoy doing together, including sex.
- We keep making decisions that are geared to produce distance rather than closeness.
- Neither of us feels seen or heard. This means being understood on the feeling level, not simply on the informational level. Being heard is the opposite of being ignored, not taken seriously, not listened to.
- One or both of us can't let go of an old resentment or many of them.
- There is no atmosphere of mended failures, so requisite to the success of a relationship.

- We keep punishing one another.
- Effective communication has become impossible because one or both of us keeps shutting the other down.
- We just won't or can't close the ever-widening rift.
- The situation does not get better even with help from therapy.
- Taking a vacation together doesn't improve anything.
- We don't really care about one another anymore.

All the signals point to our letting go rather than trying to get something to work that won't. We accept the fact that some things can't be changed. We exchange our staying put for going on. We keep opening to the wisdom to know the difference. Such wisdom happens when the "go" we have been describing in this book is not only about "going on" or changing an address. It is also the "go" in "let go."

FOUR

Working on
What Can Work

Everything comes down to loving and not loving.
This darkness will go.
Then we will have work to do, tedious too.
Finally the swan will spread her wings.
—Rumi

IN THE LAST CHAPTER we explored how and why we might leave what still has the makings of workability. This is not staying long enough to see what can be refreshed or restarted on a more even keel than we ever imagined possible. Now we look at what can help us do what it takes so our relationships and any other situations can get on track. This is staying long enough to reinvent ourselves and our connections. Being in a relationship or any commitment is not like owning a vase of dried flowers requiring no upkeep. It is like gardening real flowers that call for constant maintenance. How do we engage in effective tending?

A creative beginning is to *imagine* something working. We begin with picturing in our minds and feeling in our bodies what success or satisfactoriness looks like. This applies to any connection: our relationship, a career, a religious or political affiliation. Our internal imaging sets an intention for external success. For instance, we see in our imagination what a healthy linking of us and others would look like.

That cameo image then provides us with optimism that it can occur. This cannot be wishful thinking, which is a form of self-deception. It is instead imaging what is possible, as athletes do to win a gold medal. The practice is imaginal, not imaginary. We are visualizing what is in us as potential, not what we are fancifully making up. Imagist poems we read or write are good examples of this style.

Recently, I gave a Zoom talk on poetry as a form of healing to the local hospital's palliative care staff. We began with a photograph of a clearing in a redwood forest. The picture showed the sun pouring onto the trees and past them to the forest floor. The sunlight also traced a natural path winding around the trees and then out of the scene. I was especially focusing on the path the sun was marking. I then spontaneously asked the participants to notice what they were focusing on. I suggested they do a one-minute meditation on that part of the image and jot down a few words. They put their responses into the chat bar so we could all see them. I did the same. To my surprise, what we wrote turned out to be, without exception, short haiku-like poems! *Just focusing on the image awakened creative/poetic sensibilities.* I had planned to ask the group to write a poem, but lo and behold, they did it spontaneously before I got around to suggesting it. This is the power of an image and our meditative focus on it. The words of the participants were spun from an experience that activated their imagination at the heart level. That imaginal space will always generate a poem—that is, a soul response.

Indeed, it is only within the imaginal and metaphorical that we locate the deepest meanings of our feelings and experiences. How can we fully or even accurately describe an impactful event using only newspaper prose? Experiences with formidable emotional timbre can be viewed only obliquely. Our lens is metaphor and imagery, precisely the realm of poetry—that domain of infinite space unfillable by words that require dictionary definitions.

Space may produce new worlds.
—John Milton, *Paradise Lost*

RESOLVING OUR CONFLICTS

What follows only works when both or all parties participate. When a conflict arises, we address, process, and hopefully resolve it together. This is our style whether in jobs, affiliations, or relationships. We are engaging in three practices: taking the bull by the horns—that is, looking directly at our predicament—being on tap to process our feelings about it and hearing the other's feelings, and then being open to resolving the conflict.

In some cases, we can only go so far as saying "open to resolving" and not "finally, fully resolving." The more intense an experience, the more difficult it is to reach closure. For example, we may do all we can to resolve a long-standing resentment based on something harshly wounding from a partner or a wound that may hearken back to childhood. However, the old or recent trauma is lodged in our body-mind-heart, and as we try to resolve the issue, a stubborn element of irresolvability remains. We may never succeed in letting it go all the way, or even know why it hangs on. We are not deliberately holding on to it. The tenacity of the resentment just does not yield to the state-of-the-art techniques for resolving issues. We are encountering the mystery of incompletion that characterizes some intense experiences. Something remains buried deep beyond our comprehension or capacity to bring closure. The word *deep* is defined as "extending inward from the surface"—the opposite of *superficial. Inward* takes us into the unconscious, the realm of mystery, hence what is not accessible to our ordinary conscious mind.

Depth also applies to immense grief. There will always be a depth of inconsolability never fully finished. In knowing ourselves, too, there is an uncharted jungle we can't enter, let alone see into. Likewise, our life's purpose on this planet holds a deep meaning we will never fully plumb. We also can't completely fathom a profound poem; not even the poet who wrote it can. It isn't only timing that holds a mysterious layer of unknowability; it is anything that has layered meanings. Our etiquette on this earthly dance floor is to go with the rhythms of the mystery, to move with the pulse of uncertainty, incompletion, unsatisfactoriness—Buddha's first truth. We don't like having something we can't control, but *it is what it is*. Those last five words have to be greeted with a yes and a profound bow. Moreover, relationships can survive quite well with some elements unresolved as long as we don't let that get in the way of loving. Such a commitment to love is what makes it unconditional.

With this in mind, we, nonetheless, engage in a three-step practice for working on conflicts at home or work or elsewhere:

- *Addressing*: To address is to take an honest look at what is happening and talk about it. We do not put it off. We do not soft-pedal or sugarcoat the issue or conflict. We do not avoid it. We admit our part in what is happening. We are looking at the issue squarely in the face no matter how truculent a frown is looking back at us. Rumi says in "Childhood Friends": "Don't turn away from what is under the bandage. That wound lets in the light." That is the light of healing. *Wanting* to see where we hurt is the path to a remedy.

- *Processing*: To process an experience means paying close attention to the feelings arising in us—and others. We express our feelings and respond to others' feelings too. Addressing examines the content, the event, the story. Processing is primarily about tending the relationship. We also make a connection between what we are feeling and how it may be reminiscent of something still unresolved from our childhood. In addition, we acknowledge our own projections onto others and onto the situation at hand. This style of processing takes the same courage as addressing the issue to begin with. We look directly and show feelings in that same way. Likewise, both in addressing and processing we are open to how others respond.

  Some of us find processing scary. We keep a boundary around what we allow others to know about us. Processing can cross that boundary. It can be terrifying for us to be known too deeply or too soon—another timing issue. Processing also necessarily involves self-disclosure, and we don't know if we can trust our sensitive hearts to someone or even anyone. Perhaps fear of closeness is precisely this terror of being fully transparent—motivations, needs, vulnerabilities exposed.

• *Resolving*: To resolve an issue takes letting go of any ego charge around it. We are not trying to get back at anyone. We are not holding a grudge or smoldering resentment. In addition, we make a commitment to some kind of change. We will act differently, more effectively, in the future. We make an agreement for improving the situation, and we keep that agreement. A value in resolution is that it is not just finding a solution. Resolving gives access to inner resources in all the players so mediation can happen. Relationships and groups have self-healing powers.

To address, process, and resolve is not only a tool for working on conflicts. It is also a way of building intimacy and tending our relationships. When we engage fully in addressing, processing, and resolving in our daily life together, we are holding one another with the five A's: "I look at what is happening with attention, affection, appreciation, acceptance, allowing. I process feelings with these same five. Now all I see and feel happens in a context of love and reconciliation." True presence is showing one another the five A's. Most people have learned ways to hide from these five ways of tuning in to themselves and the experience of others. For instance, some people want to concentrate on telling *their* story, or showing how right *they* are. This content orientation dodges focusing on the feelings, needs, memories, beliefs, and unresolved issues in the room.

When any of the five A's are lacking, we may feel pain. This pain shows itself differently in each of the five. The lack also applies to childhood experiences when we may have felt similar pain regarding each of the five A's:

ATTENTION: we are unheard, invisible, unimportant.

ACCEPTANCE: we are being rejected and shamed for who we are.

APPRECIATION: we are being taken for granted, expected to do what is actually freely given by us.

AFFECTION: we are physically ignored, or we are being used for the pleasure of the other without a sense of mutuality in the transaction.

ALLOWING: we are being controlled or manipulated.

We have to beware, with regard to these forms of pain, of seeing ourselves as victims when others do not give us what we need. What helps us avoid turning into victims is greeting others' limited capacity to give with compassion toward them rather than with resentment or judgment.

(As an aside, those of us who had a sibling arrive after us might have noticed this experience when we were suddenly receiving only half the attention we had before. We didn't realize that actually the attention had all evened out since we had been getting double what we needed before he arrived!)

Let's look at three honest questions to ask ourselves when misattunements and deficits occur in our relationships. They can also apply to any frustrations we feel in life:

- *Why has the response of this person taken on such importance? Am I, for instance, trying to fulfill an unmet need from childhood?*
- *Am I encountering limits that can be givens of any human and do not really refer only to me or the strength of our relationship?*
- *Is the best path in this situation getting my needs met as I want them met or reconciling myself to the only dividend this person—or situation—can offer, however limited?*

Let's look more extensively into processing. Content refers to what happened, the story; process is about the feelings associated with what happened, the deeper meanings in what happened. Content is about events; process is about relating. It includes tracking and creating space for the here and now experience, whatever it may be, e.g., a problem or concern. This focus on the present does not discount the past, but only keeps it to one side for the moment. Here is what the two elements of processing may look like in a relationship or in any interaction:

Tracking means paying close attention and carefully following what each of us says as well as what is unsayable, hinted at but not spoken out loud. We are noticing what each other's body language is revealing about our feelings. We listen for the metaphors and images that help us enter the inner life of one another. Tracking is attentiveness.

Creating space means welcoming someone's feelings with empathic attunement, showing a caring connection to the other person who is in the room in the here and now without judgment or any push to fix, solve, advise, or criticize. It is being present with the five A's of attention, affection, appreciation, acceptance, allowing. This is how processing becomes relating.

Processing by both tracking and holding space focuses on:

- Feelings, with attention to where they reside in the body
- Feelings arising from needs, especially needs for attachment (connection) and attunement (having our needs greeted with understanding and welcoming)
- Feelings that are familiar from the past, either from early life or recent times
- Feelings arising from beliefs, projections, transferences, expectations
- Feelings showing unresolved issues including trauma from the past

Regarding feelings, we can keep in mind that most of us use that word loosely. Examples of actual feelings are sadness, joy, anger, fear, shame. There are other words that seem to be describing feelings, but often they are used as judgments on ourselves or others: isolation, rejection, abandonment, hurt, having a sense of guilt, neediness, confinement, stuckness, loneliness, being excluded. Here is an example of how the word *rejected* is a judgment of others and ourselves: "Since I am/feel rejected, I judge that others are to blame for being unkind to me, and I am to blame for not pleasing them enough."

The feeling-seeming words are important and useful. They help us define nuances in our actual feelings. They denote felt *senses*, very precise ways of experiencing a particular feeling. Notice, by the way, that the feeling words are mostly from the rugged Anglo-Saxon roots of the English language while most of the judgment words are from our more sophisticated—yet valuable—Latin/French additions as of 1066.

The opposite of each of the feeling-seeming words listed above is not a feeling either: togetherness, approval, fidelity from others, nurturance, innocence, fulfillment, freedom, movement, accompaniment, being included. *Each of these words is a way of experiencing one or more of the five A's*—e.g., the sense that we are included is related to the sense of belonging shown by acceptance of us by others. Our sense of freedom to move is associated with the A of allowing—not meaning "permission to choose" but "backing up our free choices."

We say: "I feel sad." When we use the feeling-laden words more precisely, we can instead say: "When I am lonely, I feel . . ." "When I am excluded, I feel . . ." "When I am included, I feel . . ." Each of these are felt senses of our experience, wrappers around more basic authentic feelings we may be avoiding. It is easier to blame ourselves for being lonely or blame a partner when we are abandoned rather than feel pure *grief*, which is always the other side of the coin of *grievance*. What lengths we go to when we flee what we need to feel!

In our processing together in relationships or in any interactions, we cultivate an atmosphere of safety and security. It can take a long time for someone to trust us enough to become ready to be open and vulnerable. We have to be willing to stay with the other for as long as it takes. Likewise, we may not trust the other, and we need to admit that. Both of us can then look for ways to build trust. That happens when there are many and repeated instances of trustworthiness on each side: We come through for one another. We are truthful. We keep our agreements. We act with integrity and love. We are committed to working things out by addressing, processing, and resolving them in any way we can.

In all of this, we remain on the lookout for times when our motivation for working things out might be a reflection of our compulsion to get things all wrapped up with a tidy bow. We don't want any messiness; we don't want any loose ends that may come back to haunt us. We don't want to have to go deeper into our feelings and motivations later on. Tidiness works in our physical space, but it is not a skillful means toward effective human relating or healthy personal growth. Our best motives for working on problems are to communicate our mutual truths and act in accord with them. Our best motive for staying with our practices of addressing, processing, and resolving is a true love that we are both committed to tending.

Giving our all without reserve in a relationship or in any life commitment is a crucial milestone on the human journey toward generosity. When we reach the point of putting wholehearted effort into what matters to us, we have arrived. The means—what it takes to arrive—*is* the end—arrival. We apply this to relationships: when we are wholly committed, in a relationship with both feet, we are experiencing a full true bond. This does not require an uninterrupted permanent wholeheartedness. That is impossible for beings as distractible as we are. We only have immediate experiences. In here and now *moments* of wholehearted commitment to intimacy we have reached its utmost goal of unconditional love. And those moments are not only all that matters but also all that is required.

Within each of us is a deeply embedded force that wants to evolve into the full expression of who we really are. We don't have to try; we are wired to continue growing in our awareness of ourselves. Carl Jung wrote: "There is in our psyche a process that seeks its own goal no matter what the external factors may be . . . an almost irresistible compulsion and urge to become who we really are." In other words, each of us wants to *happen*.

Accompanying one another mindfully—that is, in pure comment-less awareness—helps each of us find out who we are in relationships. This is more than personalities contacting; it is soulful communing. Communion happens when both or all parties say yes to the "irresistible urge" to be ourselves with equal enthusiasm for helping others follow that same urge in themselves. This authentic embrace lets us meet at the soul level.

Our mindfulness style of relating with soulful presence means that we become witnesses, not judges of ourselves and others. We come to trust that *staying with* feeling-laden issues will open into personal and mutual understanding. It is natural to want to fix a problem right away, avoid messy feelings, find ways of avoiding processing. Yet, deepening the togetherness experience is more likely to happen in the sheltering space when there is no dualism but only one unfolding flux of awareness.

PEEKING BELOW THE SURFACE: REASON AND REVELATION

Gertrude Stein has said things tonight it will take her years to understand.
—Alice B. Toklas

We have been looking at how some deep experiences do not yield to full resolution or closure. Let's keep this element of mystery in mind as we look into our motivations. They can fall into three categories:

LEVELS OF REASONS FOR WHAT WE DO OR DON'T DO	AN EXAMPLE: WHY I AM LEAVING YOU
The given reason (surface reason)	"You are having an affair."
Reasons that we would have to delve into in order to figure out our deep-down real motivations	"I know there are deeper reasons having to do with the nature of our relationship in general that I can't define now but I could explore sometime."
Indeterminate reasons too far into the unconscious or too mysterious ever to know	"There is just something that doesn't work and never has, and I can't put my finger on it."

Most of us don't want to go beyond our given reason on the most superficial level. Depth perception is intimidating; we fear seeing what we can't handle seeing, aren't ready to see. We know that there are levels of motivation for most choices, conscious and unconscious. At 10:00 p.m., alone in the house, we want a snack. Our conscious motivation is hunger or a desire for sweets. But that may not go far enough. Our unconscious motivation may be much more weighty: relief from boredom or loneliness. The cookie is more than chocolate chips and dough. It is a medication for self-soothing. There may also be something going on in the larger orbit of our life that this behavior contains but it is unreachable.

The conscious explanations for what we do will only scratch the surface. Below the surface is the deeper, more revealing meaning. By definition what is unconscious is inaccessible to our conscious mind. But let's not be stopped by that. There are some truths about our motivations and choices that are not known in the moment but are not buried in the unconscious. They are closer to the surface and ready to be known. So we can indeed access them by exploring our feelings and sensations in the moment. For instance, when we want the snack at night, we can look at our level of boredom. When this becomes a personal practice, we no longer fool ourselves. There is also no need to know more about whatever enigma lurks beneath it all. Our psyche wisely protects us from too much too soon. As we take on the task of becoming more aware and more resourceful, we come to see more and more of what is as it is. In the psychological realm this can train us into an in-depth view of our motivations.

There is a practice that can help us penetrate levels of self-discovery. In our journal we can respond with total candidness to four questions and ponder each in turn:

- "What am I *needing* right now?"
- "What am I *fearing* might happen?"
- "What do I hope to *gain*?"
- "Is there a loss bidding me to *grieve*?"

The first three questions help us identify our real needs, fears, and motivations. They underlie our choices and behavior. The fourth question shows us what has been lost, what we thought was coming to us but didn't, what we have been missing out on, what we expected and never received. All four of these are components of in-depth looking. Each of them can help us explore terrain in ourselves, and in our relationships at home and work, that may surprise us.

Here is an example. We are afraid of diving into true closeness in our relationship. We ask ourselves why and reply that we are afraid of losing our freedom—the surface reason. Yet with some digging, we come to see that we are actually afraid of becoming vulnerable. This leads us to realize something perhaps for the first time: we don't truly trust our partner. Our motivation for distancing is to avoid what we see as a danger rather than simply fearing the loss of our liberty. In fact, that given reason may not figure in at all. Our real issue, the in-depth reason, is about trust—why it is missing, where it went, how to find it again. The in-depth reason might also be about fear of losing our own autonomy—also a trust issue but this time about not trusting ourselves.

All four of our practice questions allow us to look under the surface into the depths of ourselves and of our behavior in relationships. But timing figures in. Someone has to be ready for revelation even if he is on Mount Sinai. It has to be our time to find out what's really going on in us before we can know. We may not yet have developed the inner resources to look directly at the full extent of our motivations. We will then, without shame, honor our timing. And we can always risk opening the door to any deeper mystery just enough to glimpse what little or more we are ready to admit.

Let's look more in detail now at investigating our real reasons and motivations. Let's use the example of procrastination about an assigned task in the workplace. Our self-given reason for our procrastination is laziness. We guess there is a deeper meaning. We go to the four elements discussed above to uncover it:

- We *need* more autonomy in our hierarchical workplace where we are low on the totem pole.
- We *fear* that completing our assignment right away would look like kowtowing. This to us means giving away our power. At the in-depth level we come to realize that our procrastination at work is motivated by resentment of authority. (Indeed, procrastination often has a passive-aggressiveness in it somewhere.)
- We see that we hope to *gain* more recognition and appreciation for what we do accomplish.
- We are *grieving* not getting so far in our job. We believe we are taken for granted. Alternatively, we might be avoiding our grief about lack of appreciation by turning it into resentment and retaliation—what procrastination can be displaying.

Now we see that the reason for our procrastination does not stop at laziness. That take on it only shows what it looks like on the surface, where no true spelunker would halt an expedition.

If the procrastinator in our example can directly admit holding resentment or having a problem with top-down decision-making, the procrastination roundabout becomes unnecessary. Knowing what's really going on puts us on a whole new highway, one with no tolls we consider unfair. With this newfound and more accurate knowledge we might find ourselves more focused in our work, more enthusiastic about projects, more apt to show initiative and inventiveness. Procrastination was never only about dawdling. It was also a forfeit of our wonderfully creative powers.

LIBERATING OURSELVES FROM TRAUMA

We move from childhood into adulthood as turtles who take their home with them no matter how far away they go. Yet, we can also be birds who fly from the nest to new worlds. Human power consists in combining the *origin* we carry with us and the *originality* we can fly into.

In the last chapter we discussed fears of intimacy. Now we look into these fears in the context of past abuses. Let's begin with a simple exercise: Close your eyes and picture yourself in a truly happy, effective, satisfying relationship. When you see the full scene and are enjoying it, bring your parents into it as observers. Note the expression on each of their faces. Then open your eyes. Was one or both of them smiling or frowning? Now you see whether you were given their permission to be happy.

A fear of closeness to others may have been an unnoticed landscape in us since childhood when our capacity to trust others was ravaged by betrayals, disappointments, abuses. Our adult conscious mind may tell us we want closeness. This encourages us to stay in the relationship. But there may be more to the story. Our whole body might still be in threat mode and on guard since childhood.

What was dangerous in our past gives us a clue about what we fear in the present. If in childhood we became used to abuse and believed we deserved it, we might believe we deserve it now. The past is always the loudest voice in the psyche. When we have a long-standing fear of intimacy in us because it led to trauma in the past, an overseer of closeness is posted deep in our unconscious—that is, in our body. This overseer keeps careful watch on any words, actions, and choices, by us or others, that might thrust us into an intimacy we aren't yet ready for. The overseer is constantly on the lookout for what might be too much for us to handle in any of our relationships, too reminiscent of a past wounding. The overseer notices every slight indication of danger and is an expert in showing us multiple forms of escape. But the "danger" here is full-on intimacy—which doesn't have to be dangerous now. The escape is direct or passive pushing the other away—which doesn't have to happen if only we can get help resolving it.

An inner sergeant at arms—body sensitivity, unconscious triggering— is constantly scanning the room for indications of authentic intimacy: giving and receiving love, risking vulnerability, showing we need someone, trusting and being trustworthy, welcoming physical closeness, letting go of ego, making a commitment, staying connected through conflicts, revealing ourselves as we really are—shadow and all. In reality none of these is harmful. They are the components of a loving bond. Embracing them can increase our love, lead us to personal growth as well as to more honesty and affection in a relationship. But at the unconscious level we mistakenly hold that these features of intimacy carry hidden perils, old in us but feeling brand new today. For instance, we fear we might be engulfed if we allow someone to get close. This fear may be traceable to early experiences of closeness that were indeed invasive. We rightly needed to escape back then. But healthy closeness can't harm us now as adults in touch with inner resources, the chief of which is openness to love.

We usually resort to the most primitive means to achieve the distance that will make us safe again: We take flight in fight. We do things to vex, exasperate, or even hurt the other. We are not really intending to be mean, but we can't seem to help it. Our shadow side takes over in order to protect us from what we fear so much: the vulnerability that happens in real intimacy. The long-distance running coach within reminds us that vulnerability was betrayed before and thus is not safe now. This is, of course, a faulty equation to the logical mind, but it is real in the amygdala. We believe we have to downgrade the level of our connection—our primitive way of restabilizing. The "extreme caution" warning about intimacy is coming from within us, intra-psychic, but it will seem to be externally caused, interactional. For instance, a partner triggers us, and we say unkind things or storm out. We are doing what the overseer recommends: sabotaging closeness, creating distance. But we blame the other person, which comes to another form of distancing. We are safeguarding our wounded hearts while starving them of the love they need.

As we catch on to what we are really up to in our dysfunctional styles of distancing, we can make amends, apologize, and finally admit to ourselves and the other person that we acted out of fear. This does not justify our aggressive behavior in the relationship, but it at least names it accurately. From such a revelation of the truth comes the possibility of healing and transformation. Likewise, an apology is a compliment, it shows the other person the importance the other person has to us, as well as the importance of our connection. Apologizing is, after all, a form of tending the relationship and doing what it takes for it to last.

By the way, regarding apologies, we distinguish between those with or without ego. An ego-saving apology is one that includes a rationalization meant to show that we were right or excusable after all: "I am sorry I did not remember your birthday, but I have been very busy." An apology that is authentic does not attempt to have us save face. It is straight-faced and heart-contrite: "I am sorry I forgot your birthday."

We might *not* do what it takes to rebuild our capacity for intimacy and nonetheless enter a new relationship. This is the work of reestablishing trust by committing ourselves to egoless honesty. We do well then at least to make a full disclosure to the new partner. An initial romantic attachment seems to promise true ongoing intimacy. We have to step in with honesty about ourselves and burst that bubble. Our disclosure will include disabusing the other of illusions: "I look like I am offering closeness, but don't misread my lovey-dovey style. I can run away or push you away once real closeness begins to happen. I have done this before and don't know if I might do it again with you. So this is fair warning. I will need help if I am to love you. Can you work with me on learning to let love in? Do you have the energy to support a scaredy-cat who nonetheless wants freedom from fear?" Yes, we can be this forthcoming. We can call our fears out. This will be a giant step toward letting them go. Healing always begins by looking at and showing the wound. We are giving honesty precedence over pretense, a courageous deed indeed.

SELF-REGULATING AND SELF-SOOTHING IN MINDFULNESS

A relationship or situation that becomes stressful can destabilize us, and we will want to flee in haste. We may be conflict-avoidant and see no alternative but escape. To stay and work things out may require a major change in how we deal with chaos. Self-regulation is the capacity to handle the whirligig of stress with equanimity. We can learn to manage our anxiety. We can persevere in doing what it takes to resolve an issue or let it go. With self-regulation we not only handle the immediate stresses. Every time we stabilize after chaos, inner unnoticed, automatic, and required fixes and integrations are happening in our body-minds. From that vantage point we perceive both what is here and the horizons beyond. We even feel a courage arising from within that will not forsake us come the next storm.

Self-regulating—and self-soothing—happen best in the context of a mindful pause between stress and response. Mindfulness is deliberate attentiveness to the here and now without getting caught in judgment, fear, or any other mind-tempting forms of distraction. We don't elaborate on our judgment or fear, but only notice them parading by as we keep coming back to our calm breathing. We do not entertain or dismiss our thoughts, but only let them flow into breaths. We are allowing a going! This is just what we want to do in a life predicament of unhappiness or unworkability.

In a mindful moment the entire Dharma is revealed. We come to see our true nature, what holds both serenity and chaos, both courage and fear. We see our nagging thoughts or negative internal messages as paper tigers, mere mental phenomena. They have no authority over our choice-making powers. Such mindful moments represent a fidelity to bare-bones reality rather than to red herrings, wishes, or thought-habits. Mindful pausing and witnessing lead to moving step-by-step through the three aspirations of the familiar prayer for acceptance, courage, wisdom. We move from accepting what is, into changing what is, into growing in wisdom about what will be:

I accept the reality of what is happening.
I do all I can to deal with this present predicament.
When the next thing happens, I will do all I can to deal with
    that too.
I will continue in this style, affirming or aspiring to the courage
    to change what I can change.
When all avenues of creating change have closed, I will say yes
    to what is.
I open to the grace to be able to do this.
I have the serenity to accept what I cannot change.
A new door, unnoticed before, will open.
It will be the gift of mindful wisdom, my true spiritual goal
    after all.

The mindful pause is beautifully ironic: We stay put in mindfulness and are thereby ready to take our next step. We have found stillness and movement, alertness and calmness together and all at once. We have noticed the illuminating qualities in our body-mind-hearts. Spiritually, this is awakening to enlightenment, the light within. Psychologically, it is the path to self-trust. Regarding the "next step," it does not always require making a plan. Sometimes, only our openness is mindfulness applied both to stillness and movement.

Mindfulness also helps us let go of ego-centeredness in our relationships. When ego is at the helm in a relationship, shipwreck is likely. We connect securely only in egolessness. Such freedom from ego opens into mindful communication:

- We state our needs without pushing to have them fulfilled.
- We state our opinion only once and let go of trying to persuade the other of our view. We are aware that every view is from a different vantage point.
- We let go of judgment while intelligently discerning and assessing. In judgment we put others down, see them as bad. This is distancing. It is also controlling since we are holding others to our own rigid standards. In assessment we look objectively, seeing both value and limitation. We share our impressions but without making others wrong. The archetype of the assessor is healthy in any of us. The archetype of the judge is only legitimate for those elected to do so.
- The main elements of mindfulness *are* the qualities of love: presence here and now, no negatives such as blame, control, or judgment, and serenity instead of drama.

Another avenue to self-soothing and self-regulation is one known in all generations and among all peoples. We humans figured out over the ages that we could offset our stresses through poetry, painting, music, dance. Yes, we can richly self-regulate through the arts. There can be a calming effect in a poem, whether it be one we read or one we write. Looking at a work of art or creating one helps us contact our heart-soul space where all is harmonious. We do not flee through art. We fly to heights no other resource can reach.

In line with art, we can recall Carl Jung, in *Memories, Dreams, Reflections*: "I learned how helpful it can be, from the therapeutic point of view, to find the particular images which lie behind the emotions." We can open to an image that may rise up from our fear, anger, sadness, joy. We use our active imagination to evoke the image that nestles in a feeling. It will not be from a book of symbols; it will be unique to us. We can practice this by dropping down into our image-making mind when we feel something. Our feeling often becomes a metaphor: "I am as nervous as a cat." Then we see the cat, notice its stance, its coloring, its look, and let it tell us something. We recall *Alice in Wonderland* and the Cheshire Cat who helped Alice when she felt frustrated or confused. Alice's dialogue with the grinning cat is a metaphor about the power of the imaginal realm: some of what we see in our minds—or in the sky—is illusion, but sometimes we hit on what is more real than real, more wise than common wisdom, and all with an enigmatic smile.

Time in nature is likewise highly self-soothing and self-regulating. Something happens when we are alone with a waterfall that can't happen in the workaday world. Something opens in us when we are sauntering in a forest that cannot do so when we are rushing through a supermarket. Something moves us to experience our own wholeness when we are standing under a rainbow or lying under a willow tree. All such moments are self-regulating and self-healing. We come to see that nature is not just a display, a set of visuals. It is a vision of what human experience and transformation are about at their sublimest level, a lens into the invisible aura that reveals and holds us. Now we know that wholeness is what happens in us when human and divine rest in one another's arms, all doubts about one another, all dualisms, dissolved.

> The natural world is a spiritual temple. . . . We walk through forests of physical things that are also symbols and they are watching us as if we were familiar to them.
> —Charles Baudelaire, "Correspondences"

MINDFULLY WELCOMING,
MINDFULLY MAKING ROOM

Everything that happens to us is an opportunity for practice, even our feelings and moods. We might run and hide from them in relationships at home, at work, anywhere. An especially powerful practice, however, is to welcome any of our feelings and moods mindfully—that is, unsullied by judgments of ourselves and rooted in the present moment. Our inner world then becomes a holding environment that fosters growth. A holding environment is one in which we can feel secure that all that we are is acceptable, all that happens to us can help us grow, all that we feel is valid, who we are is not something to be ashamed of. This is the atmosphere that fosters transformation. *Holding* in this context does not mean holding on to; it means making room. As in our early childhood when the external holding environment was not meant to keep us at home but to prepare us for our journey out of it, likewise, in this practice, internal holding is a place to find room and from which to welcome change. The more we accept our own present reality—that is, gently welcome and allow our own resistance, for instance—the more likely are to work through it. We see the paradox here: we welcome in what we closed off because it was unacceptable and it becomes something more open. What we hold nurturantly, as in the metaphor of pregnancy, ushers in a birth.

Here are the three steps that help us cultivate an inner space-holding environment, one that soon becomes a releasing environment:

1. We are mindful witnesses, rather than victims, of all that happens from people and events.
2. We welcome all we feel and experience without shame or judgment.
3. We trust that we have a capacity to make room in ourselves and accommodate our feelings and experiences without being destabilized by them. In other words, we trust what happens.

These three steps place our feelings and experiences in the roomy container of healing. Thanks to this spiritual practice, for example, we are no longer simply at the mercy of feelings, negative experiences, depression. Each has become a vehicle of integration. Each has become a friendly, assisting force in our work on our predicaments. We have placed all our feelings and experiences in the welcoming and spacious environment of spiritual and psychological health. Here is how the practice can work:

- We sit with what is happening rather than run from it.
- We allow the full brunt of our experience rather than avoid or sugarcoat it.
- We ask what it wants of us rather than shutting it down or running from it.
- We greet what happens or what we feel with each of the five A's: we are allowing it into our experience, paying attention to it with an engaged focus, appreciating its value, granting it full acceptance, and holding it affectionately. *These five practices are also the components of healthy self-love when we apply them to ourselves.*

Soon enough, this practice turns what seems like an opponent to fear into an ally to trust. We have become self, other, and event-including. That spiritual hospitality begins to illuminate us and our world. We are letting the light through. We are *presencing* our present reality. In fact, presence is just such a welcoming with open and fearless arms. We are bringing all we feel or experience into a heart-space. We are loving ourselves because we are espousing our own reality in an open partnering way. There is no blocking or dodging. Paradoxically, with no defense we feel safer: When "I walk through the dark valley," I notice that thereby "I fear no evil." There may be evil out there, but no evil we have to fear. We are shepherding, tending ourselves.

But wait, there might also be hailstones the size of golf balls coming at us. Are we supposed to allow them to pelt us? Vulnerability and openness are not always safe. For instance, we run a risk when we take on the suffering of others so much that we lose our own boundaries or crash-land with them. In that instance we are destabilized, and we won't be useful to anybody. (Our healthy response to the hailstones, by the way, is to take cover not stay put!)

We can use some affirmations to help us in this practice of turning whatever happens into something useful for movement, change, and spiritual growth. We do this because we have become alchemists turning leaden feelings and events into golden opportunities. Indeed, any unlikable trait in our personality, any choice we now regret, any hurt we can't forget, all can become all gold.

Rewrite the following declarations in your own words. Write one out each day or week, and place it where you will see it often—for example, on your computer, mirror, phone, in your purse or wallet. Repeat it aloud or internally throughout the day. You can also read the whole list onto your phone and listen to it daily.

- As I face things as they are, without self-deception or wishful thinking, my predicament discloses a path.
- I begin to see my next step and notice I have the courage to take it.
- I let go of expectations; I acknowledge reality: "I went in with no expectations, and they were all met."
- I am choosing to have no escape hatch.
- I am not trying to fix or control the situation I find myself in.
- As I let the chips fall where they may, I find ways to make the best of how they land.
- My yes to what is, and to how I and others are, has become unconditional.
- I notice that as I accept how others are and how I am, I no longer judge myself or others. Opening to my yes of welcome cancels my no of rejecting.

- Now I want to find in what happens to me a welcoming grace, a gift from the sacred heart of the universe, a light that will not go out, something enfolding me and unfolding in me.
- I trust that I have inner resources to see me through this and any predicament.
- May all people find this path to healing and hope.

Since everything that happens to or in me,
without exception,
offers an opportunity for progress on the spiritual path,
reality itself is holy.
Every time I face life as it is,
rather than deny, avoid, or oppose it,
I am in touch with the divine in me and all around all of us.

In a transitional space, a liminal space, a threshold, we are neither here nor there. For most of us, our sense of stability has been predicated on being either here *or* there. Yet, allowing instability will be necessary to move into the next chapter of life, to continue the journey a lifetime was meant to be.

In a sense then, chaos is a necessary part of the path to full becoming. This is the paradox of evolution that it generates new order from two sources: the end of the old and the chaos that follows it. We come from that skirmish to a better goal than stability. It is harmony—what synthesis is really about.

We smile to realize that, in fact, we are here on the planet precisely because just "what was" turned out not to be enough. Our family, without us, was not complete. Matter, at the big bang, was not satisfied with itself. It wanted something more: consciousness. Using a traditional religious metaphor, we can say God wanted an "other" so God created a world. But even that was not enough, so along came Eden and us—and that has made all the difference.

Tempests never reach into that serenest heaven within where pure and perfect love resides.

—William Backhouse and James Janson, *A Guide to True Peace*

PRACTICING LOVING-KINDNESS

Welcoming and making room are nothing less than love, the supreme path to the courage to stay with what can work. Courage thrives when we live in accord with core values no matter how others behave. It is a commitment to take the moral high ground in all our interactions. Love thrives when we honor caring connections in relationships, work settings, affiliations, and any program we are engaged in. When conflicts arise, we stand in them upheld by love and showing love to those around us. With a motivation to act with loving-kindness, we are no longer driven by a self-centered or fearful ego, deadly enemies of intimacy and of camaraderie. We have canceled our subscription to love-negating mindsets. The same realization that Copernicus came to has happened in us: ego is no longer the center around which other people are satellites. We have embraced a new way of being in the world: munificent loving-kindness. This practice rounds out our commitment to do what it takes to stay with what can work. It is far-reaching, farther than just ourselves, where love loves to take us.

Loving-kindness helps heal our conflicted relationships, our struggling affiliations, our compromised connections. It is a way of tending each of our frayed bonds with generosity and caring. Love is generous when it does not insist on reciprocity. The self-absorbed ego insists on entitlement to equal love in return. It is certainly natural to look for reciprocity when we act generously or show love to others. We can't, however, *expect* reciprocity. That would be quid pro quo, the opposite of unconditional love. It would also be contrary to the given of life that some people don't reciprocate or even appreciate. Likewise, insisting on reciprocity makes love and generosity maneuvers to gain a response.

We are virtuous when we let go of strategizing. We love because love is our life program not because we might thereby gain. We recall lines from "The More Loving One" by W. H. Auden:

If equal affection cannot be,
Let the more loving one be me.

Ordinarily, in relationships or affiliations that we want to run away from, our focus is on how they don't work for us. We are in despair because we don't see or even imagine anyone changing. The practice of loving-kindness refocuses us on a wider screen. It is about our loving all beings no matter what. This universality and unconditionality release us from our concentration on the inadequacies of the people around us. Loving-kindness is a practice that frees us from that narrow bandwidth. We come back to what *can* work with fresh eyes, a wider perspective, a new trust in ourselves. We now see others as redeemable, and love is redeeming them before our very eyes. We have found the central power of loving-kindness. The wider our range of loving, the more willing we become to work on the effectiveness of a relationship, or of any workable connection, here and now. Loving-kindness toward ourselves is staying in what can work and moving on from what can't work. In that sense, this entire book is about practicing loving-kindness.

We can learn to practice loving-kindness in a basically Buddhist style. We acknowledge that our love is not circumscribed by our circle of loved ones but opens into six concentric circles of relating. The first contains just ourselves, a worthy object of love. The second is comprised of our near and dear: family, partner, friends. The third is neutral people: neighbors, storekeepers, acquaintances. The fourth consists of those with whom we have difficulty: enemies, people we don't like or who don't like us. The fifth circle is not in the traditional Buddhist practice. It is one I added now that I am more conscious of racism and xenophobia. It is all those whom I see as different—that is, other than me, not like me. The sixth circle is global, all beings everywhere. In this final one we expand our reach of love far and wide. We love without reserve or exception. The farther our love goes, the bigger our heart becomes. Thanks to our practice of loving-kindness we become globe-size not ego-size.

The practice can be done daily. We aspire for what we believe is most valuable and beneficial to us and others, e.g., happiness, freedom from pain, enlightenment. We beam out an equal love for all the circles, though we don't show our love to them in the same ways. This practice extends our reach of love as goodwill toward all people. Here is an example of what the loving-kindness practice can sound like, spoken aloud or silently:

May I be happy.
May those I love be happy.
May those toward whom I am neutral be happy.
May those with whom I have difficulty be happy.
May those I see as different (or other) be happy.
May all beings be happy.

We then repeat the list substituting "free of pain," "loving and loved," or any positive phrase we choose.

This practice can also be adapted to the way we use affirmations or prayers: We don't stop at: "I am letting go of control and finding my real power." We repeat our affirmation, beginning: "May those I love let go of control and find their real power." We repeat the affirmation/prayer in each of the other five categories. We are no longer presenting only our own needs; we are widening our concern for the same needs in all people. We are no longer aspiring only for what we want; we are including all those who may need it too. We ourselves have thus become bigger or, rather, are allowing the full expansiveness of our soul to fan out to the world around us.

Here are more specific examples. We are suffering from depression. We affirm: "My depression lifts a little more each day." In accord with our loving-kindness practice, we are aware that there are depressed people all over the world. We add: "May depressed people everywhere have their depression lift a little more each day." Now we experience our depression not as something we suffer with alone but within the family of humanity. We are held in a community, and we are holding that community in our own heart. Something about that connectedness helps us—and everyone.

Likewise, if prayer is part of our practice, we can widen its reach in the same way. The doctor tells us we have a serious illness. We pray: "God help me find healing." We then add: "God help people everywhere on earth who have my same disease." As we grow in spiritual consciousness, no affirmation or prayer is limited to our own concerns anymore. We affirm and pray within a larger orbit than our own little room. In "The Good Morrow" a poem of John Donne, we hear: "Love . . . makes one little room an every where." We have moved into our real home, its perimeter planetary.

Flavius Josephus was a Roman Jewish historian of the first century. In *Contra Apionem* he wrote: "I suppose it will become evident someday that the laws in the Torah are meant to lead to a universal love of humanity." Josephus shows the scope of mature religious practice, no longer limited to any one people or tradition, let alone to ourselves. His universal consciousness can apply to all our practices—physical, psychological, and spiritual. In fact, his words can become a statement of our life purpose: "a universal love of humanity." We evolve *so* all can evolve with us. This relates to what in Buddhism is called *bodhicitta*, enlightenment that does not stop with us but embraces all beings. In other words, we came to be for beings. "I suppose it will become evident to me someday that my lifetime is meant to lead to a universal love of humanity." A Zen master was teaching archery to a student. They were standing on a cliff overlooking the ocean. The master faced a target several yards ahead of him. But instead of aiming at the target he lifted his bow and shot his arrow into the vast ocean. He then turned to the student and said: "I have hit the target." The cosmic arc is the one we honor best in any form of love, the target of a lifetime.

What leads us to practice loving-kindness? We might be drawn by teachers whom we seek to imitate such as Buddha or Christ or any other exemplars of virtue. Our practice does not waver when people don't practice with us, when they call us foolish, or when they step on us as they claw their way to the top. We are not using spirituality as a strategy to win, gain, be superior, or even safe. We are engaging in it, being it, because it is our only option now that we have seen the light. That light is the wisdom that arose in our hearts from acceptance of "what is" joined to the "courage to change it" wherever possible. Love makes all possible.

Committing to a style of love in the world may not be a difficult or uphill task we force on ourselves. We can be drawn to a life of loving-kindness in an enlightened moment—that is, by grace. Our commitment can also be something we move into gradually by the sincerity of our practicing. In this instance, we don't wait for an awakening; we awaken *by* our practices. They reflect what we are at our best, what is always in us. We feel a giddy joy in making such a transition into wholesomeness. We are actually discovering our true nature. We have become Buddha in this lifetime, our whole destiny fulfilled.

We are acting with loving-kindness, mindfulness, and integrity, without even thinking. They have become automatic, part of our profile in the world. The ancient Roman philosopher Seneca noticed this same transition: "My goodness now requires no thought but has become habit and I cannot act but rightly." Likewise St. Augustine says: "Love and do what you will." In other words, once you are truly loving, it is unlikely you will do what isn't beneficent to yourself and others. This commitment to loving-kindness highlights the ethical dimension of our practice.

The personal, as we saw above, opens into the social. Our commitment to loving-kindness lets us hear our calling to cocreate an environment of justice, peace, and love. "Hear our calling" is a metaphor for responding to the deepest sense of who we are and what we can make of our lives. Our calling will be the meeting point of our talent and what gives us bliss. We have what it takes, and we love doing it. That combination helps all the people on our loving-kindness list. Our contribution happens in our own unique way and in accord with our own timing. For instance, we may feel called simply to be there for others at first, and later to be heroic in our generosity toward them. Then we have moved from spirituality to sanctity.

In any of this, we do not look for praise or recognition from others. We have come to agree with the old public school adage: "Virtue is its own reward." Yet, we are nonetheless grateful when others acknowledge or appreciate us. We notice that we are more connected, that we care more deeply for others and for a wider range of others too, worldwide in fact. We are committed to bonding rather than to self-promoting. We are saner in how we relate, eschewing drama and not instigating or being triggered into it. All this makes us like ourselves more—that is, grow in self-esteem. All this makes working on what can work our central focus. Seeing ourselves so sincerely committed is our totally satisfactory reward. As Zen master Dogen said in *Treasury of the True Dharma Eye*: "They [ancient bodhisattvas] did not expect a reward. They were motivated by their commitment to performing beneficial actions."

Loving-kindness is a commitment to love that is unconditional and universal. It moves in three directions: self, others, all. We engage in personal change, we act kindly in how we behave toward others, and we become lovingly caring toward the world around us. Now we activate the substratum of love that is in all of us. This is how the individual love in each of us shows human connectedness already in place everywhere. This is how loving-kindness in daily practice makes us likely to stay long enough in a relationship or affiliation that can work today.

Our main focus in this book has been on our own concerns, how we might stay or go. Yet, sometimes we see those we know or love staying too long or not long enough. We are sure that the time is right for them to stay or go. We counsel, perhaps even prod, our children, friends, partners, workmates, confreres. We are sure we see their situation and remedy so clearly. A more compassionate and respectful practice for us is a mindful letting go of judging and advising. We do not attempt to move others up to what we consider our level of wisdom. We make ourselves present to them as advocates so they can take *their* next step from where *they* are, even if it is a baby step.

> May I show all the love I have
> In any way I can
> Today and all the time,
> To everyone—including me—
> Since love is what we really are
> And what we're here to show.
> Now nothing matters to me more
> Or gives me greater joy.
> May all our world become
> One Sacred Heart of love.

A WEEK OF MEDITATIONS ON STAYING

A final practice is to meditate on one of these quotations each day for a week and respond to the questions in your journal.

Sunday

> We start by making friends with our experience and developing warmth for our good old selves. Slowly, very slowly, gently, very gently, we let the stakes get higher as we touch in on more troubling feelings. This leads to trusting that we have the strength and good-heartedness to live in this precious world, despite its land mines, with dignity and kindness. With this kind of confidence, connecting with others comes more easily, because what is there to fear when we have stayed with ourselves through thick and thin? Other people can provoke anything in us and we don't need to defend ourselves by striking out or shutting down.
> —Pema Chödrön, *Taking the Leap*

How can I lovingly embrace myself just as I am?

When my relationships hit on troubled times, how I can I commit to working things out?

Seeing how hard it is to live in the world happily all the time, what would it take to let that be alright with me?

What are the opportunities for enlightenment being offered to me in my present life, relationships, and situations?

How do I stay, or not stay, with myself and my connections "through thick and thin"?

When I am triggered by what others say or do, how do I react? How can I respond with strength and confidence?

What are some ways to give up defending myself?

Will I ever be triggered by what should startle me most: how big and far-reaching my shadow side is? Self-deception keeps me highly aware of it in others but oblivious of it in myself. Let me reverse that.

Monday

New experience has become more secure than security.
—Daniel Lindley, *On Life's Journey Always Becoming*

What in my daily routine has become no longer interesting or enlivening to me?

What new ideas are percolating in my mind?

How can I put one, or some, or all of them into practice?

What has been my most recent new experience, and how have I integrated it into my life?

When I think of myself as a child, what were my trusted sources of safety and security?

How did new experiences in childhood feel to me? Were they scary or challenging, repellent or inviting, and how so?

What inner resources can I call upon in myself to create my own
safety and security?

How can I ask for some support and encouragement from others
or from a higher power so I can trust myself more?

Tuesday

Every once in a while I think of my death and I wonder how I will
be remembered. I hope my eulogist won't mention my Nobel Peace
Prize, my education, my other awards. . . . I want to be remembered
as one who tried to love somebody. Let him say: Martin Luther King
tried to feed the hungry, to clothe the naked, to visit the imprisoned,
to help the blind see and the deaf hear. . . . I have nothing to leave
you, no riches, no luxury. All I leave behind is a committed life.
Jesus, I don't want to be on your right or left side because of fame
but because of love.

—Martin Luther King Jr., last sermon as played at his funeral

How do I want to be remembered?

What do I value most and how do I act on it?

How can love be more and more lively in my life and
relationships?

Do I trust my capacity to love in forgiving ways?

What have my relationships taught me about love as a caring
committed connection?

Am I still trying to work things out with people or have I given
up? What are examples of this in my behavior toward others?

How can I open myself to joy in simple things rather than make
things complicated?

How can I more clearly see that my work on myself and my
relationships contributes to the world around me?

What will I leave behind?

Wednesday

The stream will flow through us, and all we have to do is consciously stay there. . . . It takes a lifetime of practice to remain in this flow more and more.

—Richard Rohr, *Everything Belongs: The Gift of Contemplative Prayer*

What is flowing in my life now as I work on my relationships
and my connections?
How can I stay with what is happening in a more and more
conscious way?
What will it take for me to trust what is happening in my life
now as a call to change and transformation?
Let me do the work it takes for this to happen.
What would it look like to abide in "what is" long enough to move
naturally into something that works better for both or all of us?
What graces are awaiting me in my commitment to do what it
takes to renew and upgrade areas in my life that need it?
How do I increase my courage to change what can be changed?
How can I believe in my capacity for making the most of what
is happening?

Thursday

I want to unfold. I do not want to remain folded up anywhere, because wherever I am still folded, I am untrue.

—Rainer Maria Rilke, *Book of Hours*

What would it take to be true to myself and work on my
relationships and circumstances?
Which of my beliefs, attitudes, and behaviors contract me, which
expand me?

What am I hiding that I can try opening?

How can I unfold my heart and mind to those I trust so we can be authentically close?

If there are few to trust, how can I expand my circle of trust with friends and relationships?

Since my being true to myself is part of self-esteem, how can I move in that direction more and more?

In total honesty I explore whether I really want to unfold as a person in relationships and situations that challenge me. I don't want only to wish for it.

How am I projecting a persona that I believe will be acceptable?

How can I be and do all it takes to unfold what in me interferes with relating to others?

How can I find the place in my heart where I am big enough to do all it takes to connect and commune?

I will write a poem about all this today.

Friday

I only went out for a walk and finally concluded to stay out till sundown, for going out, I found, was really going in.
—John Muir, *My First Summer in the Sierra*

When I am in nature, how can I listen and look with curiosity at all I encounter there, learning about my own life and relationships?

How are the outdoors showing me that life renews itself by ongoing cooperation?

How can I find a metaphor for my own life in the things in nature? For example, the four seasons might reflect the chapters in my own life, continuously repeating themselves.

Trees reach up to heaven and are rooted in earth. Can that be a picture of myself, both grounded and spiritually rising?

How can I open to my work of healing my relationships and
circumstances through my experience of replenishing myself
in nature?
How do the moon, the stars, and the sun help me?

Saturday

Our real journey in life is interior: it is a matter of growth, deepening, and an ever greater surrender to the creative action of love and
grace in our hearts.
—Thomas Merton, Circular Letter to Friends, September, 1968

Has "moving on" meant something only exterior or can I now
trust my calling to embark on an inner journey?
What will help me trust ever-expanding resources that are
blooming in me so I can heal myself and my relationships? Let
me trust that nothing hobbles me, nothing stops me.
How can I recognize and respond gratefully to "the creative action
of love and grace" in my heart?
How can I act from, with, and because of heart—that is, with a
commitment to loving-kindness—in all my choices?
What is growing silently in my heart that wants to expand and
hold the whole world?
How is my body opening to a spiritual power joyously moving
through me?

Month by month, things are losing their hardness; even my body
now lets the light through.
—Virginia Woolf, The Waves

FIVE

The Mystery of Timing

If it be not now, yet it will come—
the readiness is all.
—Shakespeare, *Hamlet*

TIMING REFERS TO the right time for something to happen. By "the right time" we mean the appropriate time, the moment in which everything comes together to make our decision or choice line up with our capacities and circumstances. Timing, like enlightenment or spring, is beyond our control. We can't just make it happen; it has to happen on its own, "in its own time."

We can distinguish gradual from sudden timing. Gradual timing refers to the completion of a maturation process. When we are infants, we survive on milk, then as we mature we can take pablum, then solid food. We are gradually ready for each when our biological clock permits. In other examples, spring, sunset, and dough rising happen gradually.

Sudden timing is a triggering event or a growth spurt not requiring a path of preparation. We fall in love at first sight. Bells going off in our heads with new ideas happen suddenly, just as they might when we are slipping on the ice. In nature, geysers suddenly gush out of earth—beyond human scheduling.

Sometimes, what we think is sudden has been cooking for a while. Change, movement, transformation are incubating in and around us all the time but sequestered from our conscious mind. In such an instance, what seems to happen "out of nowhere" has actually been in the works behind the scenes. Consider the humorous analogy of toys made by the mythical elves in Santa's workshop. The elves have been working industriously since December 26 on new toys. Yet, to the children receiving them it seems they "happen" suddenly on Christmas morn. Likewise, a series of synchronicities may now be afoot that will end in a "sudden" surprise meeting with our future mate, benefactor, or nemesis. From a spiritual point of view we are evolving into our full spiritual consciousness and powers in this same combination—with aid from beyond ourselves: Something, I know not what or how or where, is always lovingly at work to make me more than I am now, to ready me for my next step, to equip me for enlightenment.

There are many uses of the word *timing*: synchronizing, tempo in music, patience in taking action, the elapsing of an interval, selecting the best moment to do something, knowing it is time to step up or down. Timing also comes into play in stand-up comedy and in acting. What we refer to in this chapter as timing is mainly the mysterious timeliness that has to click in for something to happen. An example, we saw earlier, is dough rising in its own time. We do our part in preparing the dough, then we honor *its* time requirements. We only wait until the time—its timing—has come. That timing is the same as the dough's completion of its gestation. It then rises to its full complement. This time it is not sudden but slow. We ourselves slowly gestated in the darkness of the womb until the time came to be born. That first nine months was incubation—nothing to do, only grow. What a metaphor this is for the times in life when incubation is exactly what has to happen, with so much patience required from us. We recall the connection between this metaphor and the idea, in chapter 1, about hanging on in suspense during dark times. Our position in the womb, suspended by the umbilical cord, was our first practice of hanging on while also trusting the possibility of something marvelous happening when the time would come. Birth followed hanging in there. And we can't overlook the myriad rebirths we have had and will have in the time left to us if only we hang on.

Sometimes timing is dependent on nature's plan. The sailors have everything shipshape, but there can be no movement until the winds and tides agree that the voyage can begin. Our efforts on the schooner may be spot-on, but we humbly have to await Neptune's timing. This is also a metaphor for grace in the spiritual life. We engage in practices of meditation, but the moment of enlightenment is not based on our time on the meditation cushion. Our practices are not maneuvers. Timing for enlightenment is based on the *gift dimension of life*, a mysterious enacting that is not responsive to our actions. At the same time, our actions place us in the recommended position for grace to come our way—no promises, of course.

The tuning fork of the universe has twanged in different keys to usher in each chapter of my life. How can I tune in to this day's graced timing?

TIMING AND READINESS

By some coincidence, I have found the enlightenment spirit within me.
—Shantideva, *The Way of the Bodhisattva*

Timing can correlate with our own readiness. In this instance, timing can be a reflection of inner preparedness and willingness. Here is an example. We may want to win at chess, but we have to put enough time into practicing before we do so. When we have honored the time it takes to be skilled enough to win, we will. Believing or wishing we are ready is not enough. Our readiness has to match the timing, and in this example that readiness refers to the time it takes to build a skill. When our skill level has reached winning status, the time has come. Our readiness is now the same as timeliness.

On the other hand, we may doubt our readiness when we are indeed ready. We may think we need more practice at chess when actually we don't. Here too, timing and readiness have to synchronize—and we have to trust the connection. In synchronization we line ourselves up with what is required or ready to happen. At a deeper level, our own readiness and "the right time" happening can be an example of synchronicity, a meaningful coincidence of timing and readiness. This is more than synchronizing. In synchronicity it is not effort and practice that matter. Something unplanned comes along that makes us ready. For example, in the film *The Wizard of Oz*, a tornado comes out of nowhere, and it readies Dorothy to arrive at her next destination. Sometimes the time comes, and we are not ready to let it in. Timing has an energy, a push, and like the tornado it may not be courteous and await our welcome. Dorothy did not synchronize with her calling; she was carried into it from beyond herself at an unexpected time. This turns out to be a grace, yet another name for timing on a spiritual journey.

When any synchronicity occurs, it will be up to us to go with the timing or not. We can't rush it; we might lose out if we decline it:

- I can't go on Tuesday, and I don't know why.
- I can go on Wednesday. Suddenly I feel ready, and I don't know why.
- It's too late to go on Thursday. I have let the opportunity pass me by, and I do or do not know why.

Synchronicity can also refer to the intersection of readiness and opportunity. There may be a coincidence we did not foresee, but it will be profitable or useful to us: We finish our degree work just as a job opening occurs in our field. The timing was perfect. We were ready exactly when the opportunity arose. Then we have to strike while the iron is hot or the opportunity might cool.

Some people have been blessed with the capacity to recognize timing, to know what will work, when the time is just right to begin a project, when something is ready to happen, when to get in on the ground floor, when the time is past. They have a knack for reading the handwriting on the wall. They can predict what will be successful. They are accurate at pinpointing a pivotal moment. There are also those who find themselves less accurate about timing, less able to work with it, not 20/20 in seeing the handwriting on the wall. Some of what we are discussing in this chapter can, hopefully, be of help. Yet, we keep in mind that there will always be an element of mystery in timing even when it comes to learning to recognize it.

Timing can also happen because we have stepped up to the plate, whether feeling ready or not. This is an intentional making ready. Thus, when we are called upon to demonstrate a new ability, we automatically become capable of doing so *by* stepping up to the plate. This can happen on our own or because of encouragement from someone assuring us we can do it, cheering us on. Our trusting-and-doing then cancel the need for a time lapse. Here is an example of readiness happening when we step into bigger shoes than we had before: We successfully completed third grade, and we entered fourth grade though we were not yet full-on fourth graders. But coming to class daily quickly readied us for a fourth grade curriculum. Yet, we would not have been ready for ninth grade no matter how long we sat in it. Using a physical example, we are not ready for a program of strenuous exercise until our bodies are ready and our minds are focused. Timing as "the right time" is inscribed both in our minds and bodies, always the two sides of the one coin of wholeness.

Here are examples of the timing being right and coinciding with our being simultaneously ready. We entertain an idea that was unthinkable before. We finally see what is really going on in a relationship or at work. We accept a difficult truth about ourselves. We plan a career or retirement and follow through. We know we have had enough in a job or relationship. We know more time is needed before we give up on a plan. We come to know or tell our sexual or gender orientation.

In all the above instances timing turns out to coincide with personal readiness— that is, our aptness, preparedness, ripeness, fitness. Here are summary examples of the connection that can happen between timing and readiness:

- Timing can be related to readiness as event to catalyst. In effect, timing—the time it takes—can make readiness possible: "The X-ray shows my ankle has now healed (has had enough time) so I am ready to walk the trail." The sprained ankle required a specific amount of time to heal, and the elapsing of time *became* readiness to walk.
- Our readiness can occur simultaneously with the timing of someone else: "Once I was ready to learn, the teacher appeared."
- A decision to go or stay has to pass the test of time. For instance, we might be waffling about something: do we want it or not? The test of time is to see if we want it, without doubting, every day, all day, for thirty consecutive days. Another example might be to work on our marriage, give it our all, every day for three months to know whether it can succeed. The number of days or months is up to us, but the test of time is crucial in our quest for readiness—and for wise choices.
- Sometimes readiness is based on capacity, which takes time to develop: For example we may have seen a film in childhood in which a character is having an affair, but we didn't understand the sexual angle—we were not old enough to take it in. When we see the same film as adults, we grasp the sexual implication instantly.
- "Doing our homework" can increase our readiness to know what is really going on. It can seem at age eighteen—just the age the government arranges for enlistment or drafting—that patriotism means signing up to participate in war. Later, some people in the service might come to the conclusion that war works hand in hand with big corporations advancing their

profits. This is not a recent realization. Here it is in the words of Aeschylus, the Greek dramatist who died in 456 BCE: "The god of war is the money changer of dead bodies."

- Readiness is directly proportional to a capability that takes time to achieve: "I can only know of my deep prejudices when I have gained the humility that allows me to admit having them."

- Timeliness and readiness can come through as graces, the gift dimension of life. Without effort on our part, without meriting, without planning, the realization or the action simply happens. Our response is gratitude. Something—we know not what, we know not how, without our invitation or exertion—is always alert to how our heart can expand, and lo, it makes it happen.*

Sometimes, we are not ready, and the timing is not right either—for instance, in a relationship situation: Our partner is cheating, and we know, intuit, guess it but don't—can't yet—know it consciously and explicitly. The ambiguity happens because we are not ready to let the information in fully. We don't blame ourselves for not fully knowing when the time is right. As we saw earlier, full knowing can only happen when we are ready to know *and* act. Then readiness is congruent to timing, the ideal arrangement. Our body-minds have to be ready to take in what might be too shocking to absorb at the present moment. This is where mindfulness can help move things along. We sit for a long time watching our mind and thereby get it ready to see what is really happening. Such true vision is only possible when the habitual layers of projection, attachment to outcome, and wishful thinking have been dissolved—just what mindfulness does for us. Mindfulness also frees us from the fear of knowing our own truth.

Likewise, it may take a long time for us to be ready to free ourselves from guilt about the suffering of the people we love. A father

---

* My book *The Power of Grace: Recognizing Unexpected Gifts on the Path* (Shambhala, 2014) may be helpful if you want to explore this topic in detail.

with an adult son on heroin goes to one family therapy meeting after another. He hears again and again that his son's drug problem is not the fault of the parents, but he does not really let in—believe—this. Then one day, he hears it once more, and suddenly he gets it. Only when the timing was right was he "ready to hear it." Once he hears it at a deep level of truth, he won't forget it. How does this happen and why? Now we see why we use the phrase "the mystery of timing." Bowing to a mystery—acknowledging it and welcoming it—helps us spiritually because we become more humble. In fact, every virtue is an avenue to readiness.

Sometimes we can't know at a deep level because we do not yet have the capacity to know in that way. We recall John 16:12 in which Jesus says: "I have much more to say to you, more than you can now bear." The disciples were not yet prepared for the lofty mystical elements in his teachings. Buddha was in a similar situation with his students. Often we can know facts but are not ready for the implications, the arcane implicit meaning they contain but may someday reveal. When we say "by and by, when the time comes," we are referring to timing, timeliness. This connotation of timing may have a layered element. We had read *Macbeth* in high school and understood only the basic components of the plot. We see it staged at age forty, and then again at sixty, and entirely new realizations come through to us. Our access to deeper layers of meaning in the play is directly connected to an interior readiness based on age and experience, all timing-bound.

The mystery of layering may combine apparent opposites. For instance, in high school Macbeth is a tragic figure who was defeated by his own ambition. At age forty we wonder if our own life choices have been like his, or we judge him for his evil deeds. But at age sixty we feel compassion for him—while knowing he acted wrongly in many ways. We have a full portrait of Macbeth—or anyone, including ourselves— when assessment and compassion finally meet. And that can take years, which is what is meant by a gradual timing for spiritual awakening.

Timing can kick in at the moment in which we behold opposites combine. In Michelangelo's *Pietà* we see in the sculpture of Mary holding the dead body of Jesus, representing both death and a promise of life, both active grief about death and silent hope for resurrection. Likewise, in nature, we certainly see the mystery of opposites combining. The carcass of a zebra is food for the ongoing life of the vulture. Winter is the end of summer but also the respite that prepares the world for spring. This stream is flowing here today. But at the same time it is also headed to the ocean, so the present is coexisting with the future. We have a transient physical body but feel "immortal longings" too as Cleopatra said. We hold the tensions of thesis and antithesis, and in time they open into a synthesis, combining both and blossoming into what is new.

Here is a chart that shows the connection between readiness and timing, based on what we have been considering so far:

READINESS	TIMING
Preparedness	Timeliness
Linear	Beyond pattern, logic, or order
Yang energy, agency, taking action	Yin energy, opening to what happens
Able to be understood	Mysterious
We make it happen, often by plan or effort.	It simply happens, often by happenstance.
Result of practice or maturation	Fortuitous or adventitious
Individuals may be ready, but have to await cultural timing, e.g., a gay couple wants to marry legally in 1950.	Society's laws and attitudes have changed in the couple's favor.

READINESS	TIMING
Responsive to coincidence	Based on synchronicity
Requires our consent	Happens irrespective of our consent
We can work toward it, or see it coming.	It can't be planned but may be anticipated or aspired to.

We hear in *Othello* how we can't think our way into timing: "Scan this thing no further; leave it to time." In Greek two words for time stand out: *Chronos* means time as duration, time passing sequentially. *Kairos* refers to opportune timing, conditions being now just right for something decisive to occur—the time for us to step up to a calling, for instance. To this we respond with alacrity, all our hesitations gone. We know it is kairos-timing when our response does not feel like a choice. Instead it seems like an alignment to what is ready to happen or even to our unfolding destiny. We did not dig down into; we slid in, were carried in, by grace. The kairos makes time a personal experience. David R. Loy in *Money, Sex, War, Karma: Notes for a Buddhist Revolution* states it well: "Time is not something external to me. Instead of me being *in* space and time, it's more accurate to say that I am what space and time are doing, right here and now."

When the here and now are all that is real, we see that a kairos-moment has no beginning or end. All time is simultaneous—and nowhere else but here. It is what Rabbi Arthur Green describes in *Radical Judaism* as: "an inner 'place' where the ordinary linear sequence of time does not exist." When time is only now, neither worries about the future nor regrets about the past can gain entry into our minds. All those have collapsed into the only-always-already-this. We are now entering the Dharma gate to enlightenment: freedom from fear, craving, and regret.

Knowing our own timing regarding life choices is a perplexing task.

Virginia Woolf, in her notes on her novel *The Waves*, wrote: "There are waves by which a life is marked, a rounding off that has nothing to do with events." For instance, the time is just right for our needing a long period alone. Yet that coincides with our wedding day. We did not read our timing accurately or obey it. We acted in accord with events that don't necessarily align with our inner timing.

In Shakespeare's *Julius Caesar* we hear:

There is a tide in the affairs of men.
Which, taken at the flood, leads on to fortune;
Omitted, all the voyage of their life
Is bound in shallows and in miseries.
On such a full sea are we now afloat,
And we must take the current when it serves,
Or lose our ventures.

This quotation reminds us that a window of opportunity can be quite limited. The phrase "take the current when it serves, / Or lose our ventures" warns us to strike while the iron is hot. We may feel regret about how we missed a once-only opportunity in our past: "I should have moved on it back then." That may not have been possible when the timing had not kicked in for us. We don't want to rebuke ourselves for dallying when the bell had not yet rung. Only then could our steed of action take off—and all bets are off too.

Finally, we appreciate that enlightenment in Buddhism is ultimately free of timing restrictions. It is always and already real in an eternal present:

This very body the Buddha,
This very moment eternity,
This very place the lotus paradise.
—Hakuin, Japanese Zen poet

HOW TO HONOR THE TIME TO GO

Timing refers to both topics we have explored—staying too long in what doesn't work and taking leave too soon of what can work. We'll look at both.

Regarding staying too long, here are some ways to open ourselves to the fact that *the time has come* to let go of what doesn't work:

- When our capacity for denial is overwhelmed by the no-longer-deniable fact of our predicament, the time has come to admit that our position is untenable. We thereby build our capacity for surrender to reality rather than be held back by our illusory version of it. "It is what it is" replaces "But maybe it will change for the better if I keep waiting."

- Occasionally we can disregard timing and "Just do it!" We can, for instance, act as if we were ready to ask for a raise at work even though we doubt ourselves or fear a negative reply. The monkey of timing has bowed humbly to the lion of pluck.

- An attitude of yes to what is ready for change is central to honoring timing. A passage from *Markings* by Dag Hammarskjöld shows this so provocatively: "I don't know Who—or what—put the question, I don't know when it was put. I don't even remember answering. But at some moment I did answer *Yes* to Someone—or Something—and from that hour I was certain that existence is meaningful and that, therefore, my life in self-surrender, had a goal. From that moment I have known what it means 'not to look back,' and 'to take no thought for the morrow.'" A big part of coming to this yes to moving on is accepting that being insecure goes with being human. It is not a pathology or a punishment. It is simply a given. The human journey means taking on the insecurity that is the badge of change.

- Someone else might defy our timing and nudge us to make a move. A kindly physical education teacher who trusts our skill level more than we do encourages us to go out for the team even though we don't feel or believe we are ready.
- Our body knows the time is right before our mind joins in. The reverse is also true; sometimes our mind knows our readiness long before our body does.
- Sometimes hitting bottom is how an opportune time reveals itself. Our practice begins with looking up from the ditch where we will espy the stork of hope.
- Any set and setting can provide the trigger by which an "aha!" can happen and a dive can be risked. This is a splendid example of the power of grace, the gift dimension of life. When we honor grace, we honor timing.
- We turn to a power beyond ego and find an inner resource that *is* that power: "With few exceptions our members find that they have tapped an unsuspected inner resource which they presently identify with their own conception of a Power greater than themselves." (Alcoholics Anonymous)

HONORING THE TIME TO STAY IN WHAT CAN WORK

Regarding relationships, jobs, commitments, location, we might be wondering whether the one we are in *can* work. Does it have a future? We can't create the opportune moment to know this, but we can open ourselves to its happening. A style that can work to move us toward knowing is mindful witnessing of all that happens in the relationship. We notice our own and our partner's actions but without judgment. For instance, we see instances in which a new partner disrespects our boundaries or is controlling. We speak up, once only, about each point, matter-of-factly, not in a blaming way. We then notice whether a change happens. We keep track of all this and our feelings about it. We share all this in conversations with our partner. We notice the response we get. We go to couples' counseling and do the work that can rally the relationship. We notice if our partner does too. We notice whether changes happen. Then, after all this witnessing, *one morning we will wake up and know* whether to stay or go. Then we will walk not jump. Our choice will feel like a happening not a forcing or even a doing. The timing gong is more likely to sound in an atmosphere of mindful witnessing and mindful sharing than in nagging someone to change for us or blaming someone for not doing so.

Here are some practices that can be of help in relationship skill-building at home or elsewhere. Each of them also shows what to look for. Each is an indicator that a relationship is worth working on:

1. We gladly give and trustfully receive the five *A*'s: attention, affection, appreciation, acceptance, allowing.

2. We are always looking together for deeper ways to feel seen and heard. We notice the interferences represented by projections and transferences. We share our feelings, thoughts, vulnerabilities candidly, and it is always safe to do so. We go beyond projection's hall of mirrors to mindful reality-based seeing of one another.

3. We design our time together so that the five basic human longings for love, meaning, happiness, freedom, and growth can be fulfilled: We open to being loved and we love. We seek and cherish meaning in our relationship, work, or an affiliation. Each of us grants the other freedom to be who we are, no shame, no inhibition. We do what it takes to grow psychologically and spiritually using the practices in this book.

4. Honoring timing refers to how one partner or colleague respects the timing of another. This takes listening at a heart level: Our listening is more than hearing. We are engaging with someone. We are deeply focused and open. We are tuning in on what the

other is saying, feeling, showing in body language. In our relationships or work setting, we are providing a holding environment in which the other person has full permission not only to say but be.

A BOOK OF HOURS

Most spiritual traditions consider timing to be beyond egoic control and even beyond ordinary human understanding. Here is an example from the Christian tradition that may help us explore our topics of timing and readiness. What follows does not have to be about belief but can be useful as a metaphor for how timing and spirituality can intertwine.

In the gospel of John, timing is presented as the opportune moment for something to happen or for a change to be made. This timing is referred to as an "hour." Thus, we find the phrases: "my hour," "his hour," "this hour," or "the hour." There are seven instances of these phrases we can ponder. Using them as examples, they help us look into the mystery of our own personal timing. We might find them useful when it comes to making life decisions or even discovering our own destiny. One does not have to be a person of Christian faith to find an archetypal, universal wisdom in these passages. Notice in what follows how the quotations move and build on one another in a journey-taking style:

1. "Woman, why do you involve me?" Jesus replied. "My hour has not yet come" (John 2:4).

   Jesus and his mother Mary attended a festive wedding in Cana, a town in Galilee (northern Israel). Mary noticed that the bride and groom had run out of wine. She felt compassion for their embarrassment. She immediately told Jesus of their predicament, knowing he could miraculously solve the problem. We notice that Mary did not wait for the right time to go to Jesus;

she *made* that present moment the right time. Can that sometimes be an option for us, for the people around us?

Jesus responded that the timing was not right for him: "My hour has not yet come." But she disregarded his statement. She turned from him without a word and asked the servants to "do whatever he tells you." He then turned water into wine.

We see in this the archetype of the divine feminine having power over timing. Let's look at an example in a pagan context. Apuleius prays to Isis: "O Holy Blessed Lady, constant comfort to humankind, your compassion nourishes us all. You care about those in trouble as a loving mother for her children. You are there when we call, stretching out your hand to push aside anything that might harm us. You even untangle the web of fate in which we may be caught, even stopping the stars for us if their pattern is in any way harmful" (*The Golden Ass*, book II).

In the Gospel story, did Jesus realize when he saw the water that the time had indeed come? Seeing is believing, seeing is timing? Mary knew his timing before he did. Sometimes the coach knows a player is ready for varsity when the player has doubts. In our own life, there are times when someone comes along who requests, convinces, forces, or tricks us into a choice we didn't think we were ready to make. It could be that we were indeed ready but just did not know it. Or it could be that timing is responsive to wise or caring voices. All this suggests how our personal timing relates to the role of others in its unfolding. Our allies are sometimes bell-keepers.

2. They tried to seize him, but no one laid a hand on him, because his hour had not yet come (John 7:30).

3. He spoke these words while teaching in the temple courts near the place where the offerings were put. Yet no one seized him, because his hour had not yet come (John 8:20).

In both these passages we see the *protective* power in timing. The enemies of Jesus were unable to apprehend him until "his hour" to be caught had come—that is, until he was ready to die. We see in this the archetype of the hero who eludes his opponents again and again. It is clear that the hero is running the show. Only when the story has evolved so far as to bring about his willingness for capture can he be captured. We see this also in the adventures of Robin Hood. He has been captured and is in prison because his time has come to be there. We notice in that story too that it is a woman, Maid Marian, who comes to the rescue. She creates the hour/timing of release. She makes Robin ready for the next adventure of derring-do.

4. "Now my soul is troubled, and what shall I say? 'Father, save me from this hour'? No, it was for this very reason I came to this hour" (John 12:27).

5. It was just before Passover. Jesus knew that the hour had come for him to leave this world and go to the Father. Having loved his own who were in the world, he loved them to the end (John 13:1).

The hero-redeemer accepts and embraces his calling to sacrifice himself for others. He is ready for the suffering it will entail. Jesus does not ask to be spared from his fate—that is, cancel the timing. He walks willingly to his destiny, the equivalent of accepting his destiny. He even shows what Nietzsche called "amor fati," love of one's fate, embracing, welcoming one's experience rather than fighting it off or running from it. This is the essence of trust in the universe or in a higher power than ego.

We see the natural conflict between accepting pain and wanting to avoid it. In this book we are looking precisely at how we can make the move out of pain into going on. But here we have a new possibility, highly spiritual, to take on suffering in order to help others, even unknown others. We do this dressed in the wounds of our own past, often a direct pathway into our calling. The suffering itself calls: "What is it, then, that inexorably tips the scales in favor of the extraordinary? It is what is commonly called vocation: an irrational factor that destines a person to emancipate himself from the herd and from its well-worn paths. True personality is always a calling ... from which there is no escape" (Carl Jung, *The Development of Personality*).

6. Jesus replied, "The hour has come for the Son of Man to be glorified" (John 12:23).

7. After Jesus said this, he looked toward heaven and prayed: "Father, the hour has come. Glorify your Son, that your Son may glorify you" (John 17:1).

The heroic journey is about movement through suffering into glory, a word that, in the Bible, signifies divinity. Through our agonies, we discover the Grail within ourselves—that is, the transcendent within ourselves, God within ourselves. It is the time for recognition that we are more than body, mind, and ego. We hold a transcendent light inside us. The time comes for that light to shine. This divine timing happens when we have honored the many hours, timings, of our life.

Each of us, like Jesus, has watched the chapters unfold. Some were appealing, some repellent, but all were necessary for the story of ourselves to be successively told, or rather, richly revealed. We are not arrogant when we step up to the full recognition of our divine/transcendent nature and destiny. All our hours were just for this. We recall St. Joan of Arc at her trial: "I am not afraid. I was born to do this."

There is a time for everything, and a season for every activity under the heavens.
—Ecclesiastes 3:1

What's Next?

WE HAVE EXPLORED three topics in this book: staying too long in what doesn't work, not staying long enough in what can work, and the mystery of timing that underlies and propels them both. Each is a challenge that comes up again and again in any human life. We saw that all three of our topics apply not only to relationships but also to jobs, locations, associations, situations—any experience in life.

Let's finally look at three exercises that can become part of our ongoing spiritual practice: letting go and moving on when we are in a situation that doesn't work, staying the course when change and improvement are possible, and fostering our own readiness in accord with the timing of the universe.

THE TWO-BREATH PRACTICE FOR LETTING GO AND MOVING ON

> Breathe in with your head moving slightly back and say or think: "Let ..."
>
> Breathe out with your head moving slightly down and say or think: "go."
>
> Then notice the slight pause that happens naturally in any breathing. In that pause simply relax.
>
> Breathe in again with your head moving slightly back and say or think: "Move ..."

Breathe in with your head moving slightly down, and say or
think: "on."

Repeat this practice three times, more if you want.

Notice that moving your head back feels like allowing something
to come in and through you. We greet this with a nod of yes,
an allowing. We move back to let in.

Moving your head forward is giving yourself permission to let go
and go on. It is also a bow, which can be directed to Buddha—
enlightened wisdom within us—or to any power you may
choose.

This practice is a body-mind experience of letting go of what has
been and a welcoming of what will be. You are sitting in the
present and moving willingly and gracefully from past to future.

STAYING WHEN THERE IS HOPE OF SUCCESS

Find a place in nature and sit there quietly for at least twenty minutes.
Consider these five qualities of contemplation to enrich your experience of this practice: solitude, silence, stillness, softening, staying:

Solitude for contemplation is not isolation but rather presence alone
along with a sense of connection with all beings. Indeed, we never sit
in meditation alone; we are one with all people who are sitting—or
suffering—all over the world at that same time.

Silence is a letting go of words, thoughts, and concepts. Sitting silently in nature, however, does not have to mean absence of sound. We
allow all natural sounds to pass by or through us without attempting
to indulge or dismiss them. In this style, silence *is* letting go.

Stillness is not immobility but inner peace. We are free of anxiety or
worrisome concerns. We simply remain on the earth quietly grounded.
We are sitting still, alert to the world moving around us. A deep tran-
quility results.

Softening is opening to what is so that we become permeable to
powers within us and around us. We are not tensed against change. We

feel a loosening, a relaxing, in heart, mind, and body. Now we can let the light through.

Staying is full presence, an abiding in the here and now, just as it is, with no attempt to learn or find anything. We trust that simply staying will open us. We will then spontaneously see what is next for us. It will appear on its own as a calling from voices within or around us. As Henry David Thoreau wrote: "You only need sit still long enough in some attractive spot in the woods that all its inhabitants may exhibit themselves to you by turns."

GETTING READY

We attune to the timing of the universe with a willingness to listen to and look at what faces us in the moment. An exercise to foster this congruence of timing and readiness is gratitude.

We look at our lives in chapters, each with the events and people that characterized them. We write these out in our journal.

We look at what we wrote to find a thread that runs through all our chapters, something that shows what we were up to. Here are some examples: trying to find someone who cares for us, seeking the fulfillment of a need from childhood, searching for a purpose in life, trying to grasp or avoid something, acting out a role, fulfilling the requirements others had of us, finding our true selves.

Once we find the unifying thread, we pay specific attention to our three themes: the times in life when we stayed too long, to the times we did not stay long enough, and the times when we did or did not act in accord with what seemed the right timing. All three will be features of the one thread.

We do not judge ourselves for anything that happened We do not blame others. We do not hang out with regret. Instead, we look for the gift dimension in each experience. We can trust there will be a benefit in all that happened. For each we say thanks. Our gratitude is for the grace that came *through* staying too long or not staying long enough.

Our gratitude is for the timing and for our readiness—or even for our lack of it. We see how the single thread was behind all that occurred, and we are thankful for that too.

Every event and character in our story has turned out to be important, even perhaps necessary, for us to face what is happening in our lives and relationships right now.

> We affirm our trust that we will change what in our lives is ready for change.
> We affirm our trust that we will stay with what in our lives is ready to become better.
> We affirm our trust that we will be on time when the timing of the universe invites us.
> The time is *this* time, the always and already now. And you are the one saying—and being—"Yes."

Past Perfect, Present Tense
A Humorous Tale

Fairy tales like those of Cinderella, Snow White, and Sleeping Beauty have given us the impression that waiting or remaining immobile would pay off. In effect, we were being instructed not to up-and-leave what doesn't work. We were likewise given the message that if we waited long enough, a rescuer would come. And, of course, that savior was a "he" and the victim a "she." In the following story, we find an alternative.

At dawn on her fortieth birthday, Queen Snow White was just emerging, heavy-lidded, from her stepmother's laboratory in the palace cellar wherein she had toiled arduously all night on a new potion that would put a stop, once and for all, to the philandering of King Charming.

Shortly after their marriage Charming began his uncharming habit of taking long trips, with destinations never named. His briefest absence was a month, the longest six months. He never spent more than three consecutive months with her at Castle Charming Snow! When Snow White inquired about these comings and goings, his replies were along these lines: "I was seeing to my far-flung lands, meeting with my overseers, selling some of my family holdings," or even this most recent time, "I was looking in far-off beanstalk country for a special gift for this, your special birthday!"

And special it was going to be, thought Snow White, as she trod the interminable stone steps back to her tower apartments. For tonight, at the banquet in her honor, he would be toasting her with a goblet of wine laced with the potion she had prepared. Its careful combination of such ingredients as tongue of magpie, blood of rat, hair of fox, and guano of bat, would put him into a trance. He then would talk like a magpie about what a rat he had been to her, now unable to outfox her radar on his clandestine escapades. He would then become ever after a dutiful husband with never another wish to go a'wandering.

All through life until now, Snow White could not let herself know fully about his betrayals, so credulous had she always been about the upright motives of others. Why else would she have trusted her stepmother in every villainous disguise in which she had appeared, until the apple of final vengeance took her innocent life. She had always somehow trusted her husband in the same way, though her deepest intuition had always told her otherwise. And as long as her denial was equal to her failure to take action, she was indeed stalemated.

Snow White's isolation and abandonment over the years certainly weighed heavily upon her. The seven dwarfs had been her support system. Of them, only one remained—Grumpy. Snow White had learned, many years ago, that he could not be entrusted with her confidences. He would invariably preach, scold, or guilt-trip her for doubting such a charming spouse who had brought her back to life and let her live happily ever after. But Snow White still loved and cherished her old and grumbly friend.

After each return of the wandering king to Castle Charming Snow, the queen had, in the early years, rifled through his saddlebags, trunks, and fanny pack, seeking a clue to the mystery of his whereabouts and his with-whom-abouts, while still hoping also to find evidence of his loyalty. Snow White was always wanting to know and not to know. In any case, she could never discover any incontrovertible proof, any truly telltale sign of sexual liaisons, no matter how assiduously she searched.

In all these years she had found only one unusual item: once, from the folds of his nightshirt, a single green pea had rolled out. "He certainly doesn't get his laundry done elsewhere as carefully he gets it done here at home," Snow White huffed and then thought no more about it.

Meanwhile, King Charming, unaware that doubts about him had ever crossed his wife's childlike mind, arose from the lowly bed of one of her ladies-in-waiting. The king had found this one's charms quite unmemorable and certainly would not recall her name—if he even knew it now. He felt quite smugly satisfied with himself that he had finally fulfilled his wish to sleep with every one of the eight ladies-in-waiting, unbeknownst to his wife. All his life, his charming looks, speech, and behavior had won Charming a facile place in the female heart. His conquests—if conquests they could be called when they fell to him so easily—were varied and numerous. Never satisfied with only one story, he had to be part of many, a visitor to one at a time, the Prince Charming of every virginal hope.

On their honeymoon, in fact, Snow White had asked him querulously why it had taken him so damn long to come and kiss her back to life. Lands, holdings, overseers—anything but reveal those ecstatic months in the arms and hair of the young Rapunzel! Charming thought to himself: *Why hurt the feelings of someone as innocent as Snow White? Why cut short his own carefree life of wine, women, and lies? And besides, to Snow White, after all his literally best lady in waiting, would he not always return?* Charming chuckled to himself about his annual private joke on Snow White: he would invariably bring back a souvenir of his most recent romance and give it to her as a birthday gift! He did this for two reasons: First, he could betray all of his lovers by stealing something dear to them and giving it to his wife. Secondly, he could clear his own conscience by subtly disclosing to Snow White that he was indeed the Prince Charming of every fairy tale, not only hers. This was his way of admitting his infidelity. Her silence in response—albeit quizzical—felt to him like a tacit approval! At noon today, he would leave his latest gift at her door, as was his usual custom.

As Snow White finally arrived this morning at that very door, her ladies-in-waiting (minus one) greeted Her Majesty with fussing about her baggy eyes and disheveled, lusterless locks. They frantically reminded her that she had to look her best for the procession from the castle to the Cathedral of Our Lady of the Snows where, in an hour, the archbishop was to celebrate a solemn high mass in honor of her birthday. Snow White then pictured the long ceremony that awaited her, the adulation of the fawning prelates and her husband kneeling so devoutly beside her. With an imperious clap, the queen shooed her maids out of her bedchamber, shouting to them as she slammed the door, "Tell everyone I won't be at the services and can't be disturbed until the banquet tonight!"

Snow White sighed with fatigue and relief. Her glance now happened to fall upon the cedar and glass cabinet made for her by the dwarfs as a wedding gift. In it, she kept some of the annual birthday presents of King Charming. The gifts had always puzzled her: a soft mattress, a pair of glass slippers (worn only once), a silk pillow on which a young woman's head had lain sleeping for a long time, a basket of straw turned into gold, a golden ball that smelled remarkably like frog. She knew that the king would soon be presenting this year's gift. Too drowsy now to speculate on what it might be, she lay across her bed, the bed on which the charms of Charming rarely charmed her. With a heart now heavy with sadness—and yes, compassion—for both of them, she fell into a reverie. In it, she found herself recalling a poem her mother had composed before she was born. Snow White had found it in an old chest and learned it by heart many years ago:

I know and do not know.
I trust and do not trust.
Each blank I fill with snow.
I barely know so cannot go.
Snowed in, snowed under,
Only a whimper, never thunder.

I guess the fullest fact,
But not its full extent.
I keep an inner pact:
The truth, but always bent.
Snowed in, snowed under,
Only a whimper, never thunder.

Pilgrim Goose, you know the way
To summer's light-filled shrine,
Come for me some lonesome day
And let your flight be mine!
Then out from under,
Welcome light, welcome wonder!

Snow White soon lapsed into a long-overdue slumber on her satin quilt. Soon in a dream she found herself staring at an old mirror. In it, she beheld not herself but her ancient stepmother! As she continued to gaze, Snow White soon noticed, with amazement, that the cruel visage of the old queen was softening with tears. And through these tears, she was looking fixedly and even kindly at Snow White. "Do not be afraid, my child. I know what you feel and how you suffer. I too was lonely in this great house while your father traveled abroad. I too never wanted to know of his secret life. I became obsessed with making him want only me. This is why I could tolerate no rival to my beauty under this roof. So I tried to kill you, to kill what he loved here. There would then be no one here to draw him home but me. My jealousy of you made it easy not to know I could never be enough for him. Oh, yes, he was man enough to win a hundred women, but not man enough to live with one! This is the castle of those who refuse to know the truth about their marriage and become hard and bitter, and you are now its queen!" As her stepmother's face began to fade, Snow White heard her whisper, "This mirror has one magic answer left in it. Ask your question, my daughter, and remember me, my griefs, and my amends to you."

Snow White was now astonished to see no image in the mirror except a prematurely wrinkled countenance—her own. From deep inside herself a question welled up: "To whom can I turn?" The mirror blanched, then became luminous with an unearthly light, and finally, responded with a single image: the perfect likeness of the little Snow White as she looked before she could pronounce the word "charming," when her musical laughter was the joy of this palace and the fulfillment of her own mother's wish for a princess with a face like snow, lips like rose, and hair like ebony.

Snow White now contemplated herself and all that she had lost. She then felt her hardness dissolve into a stream of tears—a grief so necessary, so releasing. And these were the tears in the eyes of Snow White when she awoke and finally, fully let herself know: "He won't ever give me what I want and need, and I will never be able to get it from myself until I stop trying to get it from him. Once he revived me; now only I can revive myself."

At the candlelit birthday feast that night in Castle Charming Snow, all the velvet purples of the nobility had gathered to honor their Royal Highness, Snow White, always to them the darling princess of their fairy tale. A famous English poet had been invited to entertain the guests with recitations of his mellifluous verse. But everyone looked in vain for the subject of their rejoicing. Snow White was nowhere among them. When a worried groom whispered to the king that Her Majesty's horse was gone, Charming hurried anxiously away from the richly laden tables and the redolent candles. As he was leaving the hall, he could just hear the poet reciting the words: "Then longen folk to go on pilgrimages . . ."

Arriving apprehensively at his wife's bedchamber, Charming found no Snow White, only a little broken potion bottle on the hearthstones and the wrappings from his birthday present on the nightstand. He sat on the bed in stupefied wonderment and chagrin. No woman had ever left him, and, of course, he could not believe this one had either—especially since she must have gone with no money.

So how far could she get? Charming lifted the box that had held his gift and noticed that it was empty. Snow White *had* taken what would allow her to live a long life away: his gift of one dozen golden eggs from the magic goose of his newest friend Jack!

About the Author

David Richo, PhD, is a psychotherapist, writer, and workshop leader. He has taught at a variety of places including Esalen and Spirit Rock Buddhist Center. He shares his time between Santa Barbara and San Francisco, California. Dave combines psychological and spiritual perspectives in his work.

The website for books, talks, and events is www.davericho.com.

BOOKS BY DAVID RICHO

How to Be an Adult: A Handbook on Psychological and Spiritual Integration (Paulist Press, 1991)

When Love Meets Fear: How to Become Defense-less and Resource-full (Paulist, 1997)

Shadow Dance: Liberating the Power and Creativity of Your Dark Side (Shambhala, 1999)

How to Be an Adult in Relationships: The Five Keys to Mindful Loving (Shambhala, 2002) (Revised Edition, 2021)

The Five Things We Cannot Change and the Happiness We Find by Embracing Them (Shambhala, 2005)

The Power of Coincidence: How Life Shows Us What We Need to Know (Shambhala, 2007)

The Sacred Heart of the World: Restoring Mystical Devotion to Our Spiritual Life (Paulist Press, 2007)

When the Past Is Present: Healing the Emotional Wounds That Sabotage Our Relationships (Shambhala, 2008)

Being True to Life: Poetic Paths to Personal Growth (Shambhala, 2009)

Daring to Trust: Opening Ourselves to Real Love and Intimacy (Shambhala, 2010)

Coming Home to Who You Are: Discovering Your Natural Capacity for Love, Integrity, and Compassion (Shambhala, 2011)

How to Be an Adult in Faith and Spirituality (Paulist Press, 2011)

How to Be an Adult in Love: Letting Love in Safely and Showing it Recklessly (Shambhala, 2013)

The Power of Grace: Recognizing Unexpected Gifts on the Path (Shambhala, 2014)

When Catholic Means Cosmic: Opening to a Big-Hearted Faith (Paulist Press, 2015)

You Are Not What You Think: The Egoless Path to Self-Esteem and Generous Love (Shambhala, 2015)

When Mary Becomes Cosmic: A Jungian and Mystical Path to the Divine Feminine (Paulist Press, 2016)

Everything Ablaze: Meditating on the Mystical Vision of Teilhard de Chardin (Paulist Press, 2017)

The Five Longings: What We've Always Wanted and Already Have (Shambhala, 2017)

Five True Things: A Little Guide to Embracing Life's Big Challenges (Shambhala, 2019)

Triggers: How We Can Stop Reacting and Start Healing (Shambhala, 2019)

Wholeness and Holiness: How to Be Sane, Spiritual, and Saintly (Orbis, 2020)